GOD UNLIMITED

IN DAILY LIVING

By the same author:

C.T. Studd, Cricketer and Pioneer

Continuous Revival

The Deep Things of God

Nothing is Impossible

The Law of Faith

The Leap of Faith

The Liberating Secret

Once Caught, No Escape (autobiography)

Rees Howells, Intercessor

The Spontaneous You

Touching the Invisible

Who Am I?

Yes, I Am

GOD UNLIMITED IN DAILY LIVING

by

NORMAN P. GRUBB

Zerubbabel Press
Blowing Rock, North Carolina
USA

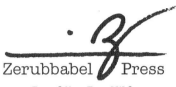

Zerubbabel Press
Post Office Box 1710
Blowing Rock, NC 28605

Copyright © 1962
Norman P. Grubb

First published 1962
Lutterworth Press
P.O. Box 60
Cambridge CB1 2NT
England

First American Edition 1975
Christian Literature Crusade
under special arrangement with the
British publisher

This printing 2002

ISBN 0-9662957-4-9

All Rights Reserved. No part of this publication may be translated, reproduced, or transmitted in any form or by any means, electronic or mechanical, including photocopy, recording, or any information storage and retrieval system, without permission in writing from the publisher.

PRINTED IN THE UNITED STATES OF AMERICA

Contents

Foreword to the 2002 Edition	8
Foreword by the author	9
1. The Ultimate Reality	11
2. God's Dilemma	17
3. The Sole Function of the Human	21
4. Man's Unlearned Lesson	27
5. God's Problem Solved	33
6. Man's Problem Solved	37
7. How Acquire Faith?	42
8. The Second Work of Grace?	56
9. A Crisis in Most Lives	64
10. Signs—With or Without?	69
11. Old Man . . . New Man	75
12. What the New Man Has to Learn	81
13. Spontaneous Living	89
14. Adversity or Adventure?	96
15. Law, not Sin, the Problem	103
16. How Does Soul Differ from Spirit?	112
17. God is Seen God	123
18. Long on Faith, Short on Love	128
19. Can We Take It?	135
20. A Man Who Lives the Sermon on the Mount	142
21. Prayer and the Fourth Dimension	149
22. The Summit	170
23. From Lowlands to Highlands in a Series of Letters	187

Foreword to the 2002 Edition

God Unlimited is the next of Norman Grubb's books brought back into print by Zerubbabel Press. Originally published in 1962, and then reprinted in 1975 and 1977, *God Unlimited* has been largely unavailable for many years. Our gracious colleagues at Lutterworth Press have been instrumental in making this endeavor possible.

As in previous reprints of Norman's work, the Editors have striven to preserve *God Unlimited* in its original form. Many different elements of style are found in the book that may be unfamiliar to today's reader. Some may come from the original editors; others are simply the idiosyncrasies of the author. Only gross inaccuracies in spelling and punctuation have been corrected.

The costs associated with publishing *God Unlimited* have been underwritten by generous contributions to Zerubbabel, Inc. and its newsmagazine, *The Intercessor*. We anticipate that you will appreciate Norman's message in this book as much as we respect the opportunity to bring it to you.

Editorial Staff
Zerubbabel Press

Foreword

I have not much to say in an official foreword, because the first chapter of this book just about takes its place. So I would only mention here the encouragement I have had to keep delving into the things of the Spirit and to put them on paper from such hundreds of eager seekers after the released life I meet, many of whom God has enlightened through the other books. Some have especially encouraged me, foremost among them, in the writing of this book as in all the others, being my beloved wife and fellow-soldier in Christ, Pauline, with whom I have shared forty-two years of missionary ministry. I thank God, too, for my fellow-workers worldwide in the Worldwide Evangelization Crusade, over 800 of them, who are patient with me as I combine this kind of extensive inner pioneering with our extensive commission to "the uttermost parts of the earth".

I am especially thankful to my wife's and my friend, Mrs. Lydia McLain, who has kindly typed this manuscript for me, as a gift to the Lord, and from whose letters I quote extensively at the end of the book. I am even bold to quote from what she writes after typing it, though it may sound presumptuous to do so, in case it might encourage some to go on reading. "The Author in you certainly has unveiled Himself in these pages. What I marvel is that the book would appeal to persons of all walks of life, to the lowest and then to the most intellectual, to the Biblical scholar and also to the scientist, simple and yet to the depths of the depths of the Spirit. You have been able to take the various beliefs of the various schools of thought, and show them in their true light right down to the roots. There will surely be those who reject the blazing light streaming from these pages exposing the ego, but to others it will be a most welcomed book far surpassing anything we have read from your pen. I only wish that such a book was put in my hands ten years ago, but perhaps God meant me to walk in darkness before allowing me to have my eyes opened really to behold Him. You did not write that book, God did in you." Strong words, too strong, but may God at least shine rays of light into hearts through it.

N.P.G.
Fort Washington, Pennsylvania, U.S.A.

Not God first
but God only

Chapter One

The Ultimate Reality

Although I am a missionary secretary, the subterranean stream of my life-interest for thirty years has been flowing in the direction of what to me is total truth. Big words, and perhaps I should qualify them by a definition that "only the truth which edifies is truth for you". After I had been a servant of Christ for twelve years on the foreign and home fields, I went through a strange phase of a kind of intellectual awakening. It seemed as though my heart had outpaced my head, and the time had now come when my understanding must catch up with my love. It was a painful phase at the beginning. I had to learn the dialectical truth that the way to clarity is through confusion. For a year I went through the strange experience of questioning whether there was a God at all (God forgive such presumption!), and found myself in the strange situation of knowing and loving One of whose existence I was uncertain! Though I decided that if He was the Big Illusion, I would be a little illusion along with Him! But what it did for me (which makes me sure that it was God who took me that way) was that it put passion into my faith. I *must* know. I *must* have sure grounds, even if those sure grounds were to be quite sure I could never be sure, but that I could and would believe!

That passionate pursuit has never left me, except that it has brought me in my old age (65) to the calmer waters of an understanding which does appear to me to be the heart of the matter and the heart of the Biblical revelation. For several years now I have been occupied in sharing what I have seen (God's seeing in me, I trust), with many others in conferences, churches, house groups, etc., and it seems to ring the bell in many hearts; nor have I found reason to change the mainstream of the message, though different aspects come clearer all the time. I have put it in print three times, in *The Law of Faith, The Liberating Secret,* and *The Deep Things of God*; but I don't know if every writer on the things of the Spirit has the same problem—no sooner have I completed one manuscript than I see this and this and this which could be put so much more clearly, or whole areas of insights which should be added. And that is the reason for this little book. I feel like the automobile dealers who *must* produce a new model each year! I should add also that, though not a wide reader through lack of time, nor having the powers of concentration of a true student, I have delved and burrowed in various directions where I have met with authors, past and present (mainly past), who have struck me as germinal, writers "piercing even . . . to the joints and marrow", and not merely proffering odd Biblical tidbits. They might make a strange array if I mentioned their names!

It seems as if we have to put things in extremes, in absolute terms as the Bible often does, to get truth to register in our consciousness. And I find there is a basic "extreme" which had to dawn as a fixation in my own spirit. I find equally that with hundreds of my fellow-believers whom I contact, few seem really to have "seen" it. Those who have not are hungry, not basically satisfied, negative and self-condemning in their outlook. Those who have know that they have "come home". They have reached ultimate reality, and though they may wander from the road as we all do, they know where to return to, and how. I have to add too, though hesitatingly because ministers cannot all be teachers as well as evangelists and pastors, that in a great many evangelical churches the gospel of salvation is magnificently presented, seekers are led to Christ; but the totality of the gospel, the gospel in its ultimate category, is by no means so clearly presented, nor maybe even understood by teacher as well as taught. It is evidenced by exhortations to Christian living being mainly challenges to pray more, give more, witness more, surrender more. The emphasis is predominantly on the active dedication of the Christian to his Lord, and to a much less degree on the dynamic remoulding of the believer by His Lord.

The extreme, the absolute, the revelation of which so totally re-orientated my own life, was the fact, so plainly and repeatedly stated in the Scriptures, that there is really only One Person in the universe, and that is God Himself. To say that sounds exaggerated, because we immediately counter it with the seemingly obvious alternative fact—that we also are persons. Yes, that is true in a purely secondary sense; but the trouble is such a totally distorted concept of the function of the human self has captured and blinded the world since the Fall that the only way to destroy the false and replace it by the true is by almost throwing out the human self on the rubbish heap, and only restoring it to its proper place when we have restored the right perspective.

The way I saw it was when it suddenly dawned on me that the Bible does not talk about God having a lot of separate gifts and graces with which He would endow me (though a surface reading of the Scriptures might appear to say He had); but it continually says that God Himself (Father, Son, or Spirit) *is*, not *has*, so and so. What you have is not you, but merely possessions you can share with others. What you are is you, and you cannot take parts of yourself and share them with others. The Bible says, God *is* love, God *is* light, Christ *is* our life, Christ *is* the power of God, Christ *is* the wisdom of God, Christ *is* our sanctification; the Bible speaks of God our hope, our peace, our exceeding joy; (the peace of God, for instance, in its hidden meaning for those who have eyes to see it, is really God our peace; and the same is true of each attribute of God, which might read as if it was just some "thing" He shares with us, but in reality is He Himself as such within us): and the ultimate being "Christ *is* all and in all" for the believer, and "God all in all" in the universe.

It was the exclusiveness of God which confronted me. I had been looking for a lot of gifts and graces to improve me as a servant of Christ. The answer I received was "Nothing doing. There are no such 'things' for you. These things are not things at all, they are all the characteristics of a Person, and only one

Person in the universe. They never can be yours. They are not available to you, nor attainable by you." That shook me, and I needed a shaking—from this mistaken concept of the position and function of the human self. I cannot be thankful enough that I was given to see this absoluteness, this exclusiveness of God. I say again, it may sound extreme, it may not even be all the truth (in the sense that we are also persons), but once and for all I had to get out of my system the idea that ultimate life is I alongside God, God alongside me. No. Life is just GOD. Not God first, but God only.

What about things and people then? If God is the All, what are things and people? The nearest we can say, as the Bible says, is that they are the means of the manifestation of God. Everything is a form of God, a manifestation of God. The visible is made out of the Invisible, as Hebrews 11:3 says (Moffatt translation). "That's a bit dangerous", a preacher said to me recently. "You mean that God made everything". No, I don't, I mean more than that human analogy by which we say that an artist is here and his picture there, two separate entities, or a carpenter here and his table there, and so in that same sense we say that God is there and His creation here. This is a different relationship. We must bridge that gap of illusory separation. We must say that everything is God on a certain level of manifestation. It is God revealing Himself in the variety of His wonders. We see God in the beauty of colours. We hear God in the harmonies of music. Nowadays we know that all the infinitude of material objects have one invisible origin. What is that origin? The scientists say that probably man can never penetrate beyond the atom to its source. But the believer can. It is a Person. Paul said it two thousand years ago when he wrote, "By Him all things consist (stand together)". Faith can know what human reason never can. "By faith we understand that the worlds were framed by the Word of God." The Word is God. He is the Word. Open our eyes then, and wherever we see things, we see Him in one form or another.

But is that not pantheism? How absurd—that God is a thing, or God is a colour, or God is a sound? No, God is The Person. A person is not a thing, but things are forms of Him. "The whole earth is full of His glory": He "fills all things". How can we but worship—everywhere—not the thing, but Him in the thing.

And people? Now we come nearer home. Paul was bold to say of all humanity, redeemed and unredeemed, that "in Him we live and move and have our being". That is a strong statement. Not just that He made us and in some sense we have a derived but separate life He has given us. No indeed. All men are *in* Him. Their natural life, their thinking and acting, are expressions of Him. It is impossible for any created being, of this world or any other, including the devil and his angels, to be out of God. All are "in Him" eternally, He is the hidden root of their lives, the hidden Self behind their selves. Separation from Him is an impossibility. But that immediately raises an obvious problem. Are evil people an expression of God? Are evil deeds His doings?

Chapter Two

God's Dilemma

We now come square up to what appears to us humans as God's dilemma. But what confronts reason as an unresolved paradox is surmounted by faith which acts on revealed facts, though often it cannot explain them: and faith is equally assured that what it now sees dimly and with seeming contradictions will yet prove to be the very summit of God's wisdom, God's artistry, the highest perfection of God's creation. A person can only be a person with other persons. We can only be ourselves with our fellows. I-Thou is a different quality of relationship from I-It. God is The Person. He can reveal His glory through other forms of creation. He can only reveal Himself, or be Himself, through selves. Person through persons. But just there arises the problem. A person is only a person by the endowment of self-consciousness, which is freedom, the created spirit made in the image of the Creator Spirit.

When we say that a person is endowed with self-consciousness, which is freedom, what do we mean? Penetrate into a self, God's self, our self, we find desire. A self desires to please itself, to express itself, and so on. How does God, the primal Self, do that?

By the begetting of His Son to be the object of His love, and the Son receiving and returning the love of the Father; and the Spirit of the Father and the Son proceeding forth to express the same love-nature in all creation. But a self can please and express itself in an opposite manner. Others can be for its benefit, not it for others. Self-loving, not self-giving can be its motivation. When we speak of a self-conscious self, we therefore mean a person capable of recognizing the opposites which are the basis of all manifested life, and who has freedom of choice. God, the Original Self, has been fixed in choice through all eternity. His self-life is the love-life of pure self-giving, for God is the Eternal Three loving and serving each other. In that sense we may say that there has been a cross in the heart of God through all eternity, for He has eternally died to the possibility of being a self-loving self, and all the powers of His selfhood have been poured into self-giving service, in which He finds the consummation of all the desires of self, "His good pleasure which He has purposed in Himself", so that He *is* joy, He *is* peace, because He *is* love.

Here is the reason that we are persons in a secondary sense. We are persons to contain and manifest The Person. All the universe contains and manifests Him as Person. But, being created in His own image, we are self-conscious selves; at our centre we are spirits, even as He is Spirit, and having the same basic selfhood as God, we are free to make the choice of the two alternatives. Therefore we have to be awakened to an understanding of how fearfully and wonderfully we are made, to be freely, lovingly, intelligently the containers of the One Person in the universe who is the God of self-giving love, Father,

Son and Spirit, so that He can express His love-nature through our natures, and we find the delight and entire satisfaction of our created natures in being as He is, living as He lives, loving as He loves. But understanding that we are free selves with our normal capacity of self-love and self-pleasing, it is fearfully possible that a decision in reverse might be made, and a tremendous rupture in the harmony of creation, by some created person choosing to follow the hitherto unknown and unexposed route of self-interest, rejecting the purpose of his creation and making his own self-sufficiency his god.

That is what we know did happen, by the Bible records of the fall of Lucifer and the fall of Adam. In this sense created beings, who are forever in God, and live and move in Him, so far as their created life is concerned, yet live lives which produce the direct opposite of God, all the evil of self-love in place of all the good of self-giving, and defiantly delight to do so. Yet they are still God's sons, as Satan himself is called (Job 1:6), and God's offspring (Acts 17:28). They are children of God's wrath, children of darkness, experiencing the reverse side of love: its hate, its anger, its judgment. And God's power in them is in reverse, giving them over to their sins, hardening their hearts, fitting them to destruction. Here is the answer to the question, Are evil doers an expression of God? Are evil deeds His doing? Yet in saying this we must still go back to God Himself in the perfection of His wisdom and love. He works all things after the counsel of His own will, Paul says, and that will is the good pleasure which He hath purposed in Himself. Only Omnipotence can give freedom, because, being Omnipotence, the freedom is still contained within it.

No one less than Almighty God can give freedom, because the free can then escape the reach of the giver. But not with God. Yet it is a paradox. That is why we said that the ultimate plan and purpose of God is beyond human understanding, and demands nothing less than the humble faith of the creature in the Creator. We humans in God's image *are* free. We know we are. We act as such. Yet in the ultimate sense our freedom is contained within the established purposes and power of God from eternity, and ultimately all serves Him and is to His glory, good and evil alike. Who can embrace that paradox? Only believers.

Chapter Three

The Sole Function of the Human

Now let us return to our main line. There is only really One Person in the universe—God Himself. The creation is the means of manifesting Him. Human beings, created as persons in His image, only exist to contain and manifest Him as The Person, for they alone as persons can do that. But likewise, being persons, and therefore self-conscious and free, they can and did refuse to "retain God in their knowledge", and thus became the containers of the false spirit of self-love in place of the Divine Spirit of self-giving. The way they became like this, and the way back, we will go into later.

But at the moment I want to stress most plainly the complementary fact to God being the only real Person. It is that we humans are basically containers, and nothing else. I have already referred to our misconception of the function of the human self, and here it is. Through the self-sufficiency we inherited from the Fall, we instinctively regard ourselves as something very much more than containers. "Vessels" the Bible calls us; it was the first description given by the Ascended Christ of the most dynamic Christian of history, the Apostle Paul: "He is a chosen vessel unto Me": just a vessel, that was all. Were all the dynamism, the wisdom, the revelations, the passionate love, the self-sacrifice then attributes of the vessel, or of Him whom it contained? And Paul himself went on to call us all "earthen vessels". Not even tin cans, but nearer to crack-pots! Humbling, self-emptying, an offense to any man not enlightened to facts by the Spirit of God. But let us get it plain, and without equivocation. If God is the All, and we are merely the means of His Self-manifestation, is it not a fact that we must be just containers? "Christ *is* all and *in* all". "Temple" is another like metaphor, for a temple has no reason for existence except to house its god: "Ye are the temples of the living God; as God hath said, I will dwell in them, and walk in them."

The point then is that a vessel or temple has only one function (and you will remember that we humans have a misconception of the function of the human self). Activity is not the function of a vessel, but receptivity. Here we reach right down to the roots. Receptivity is the simplest, most child-like human function. In Bible terms, it is not works, but faith. But what we have to re-learn is that receptivity is not *a* function, but *the* function. All other functions are by-products. The whole of life is a parable of this. Is not everything some form of the self-giving of God? And do we not totally live by what we receive—food, air, the floor boards beneath our feet, the clothes on our backs? And in most cases something has died to give us life. Life is surely based on receptivity, and the Bible word for receptivity is faith. Can anything be simpler? How wonderfully God has made us: to live, spiritually and materially, by exercising a capacity which is as near as possible to doing nothing—just receiving. Not reaching up to drag things down, but things poured upon us in such abundance that we just open our mouths and they are filled: and the gift of gifts we receive is Himself.

Wait a minute, you may object, but we do have to act also. Certainly, activity is a product of receptivity, but not a substitute for it. But remember we said that we must take extreme measures to expel the human self from its false position before we can replace it in its true one. Certainly, we are real persons. We think, we will, we act. Yet it is not safe or even true for us to regard ourselves as such until first we have "died" to our independent selves, and begun the life of constant recognition (reception) of Another as the Real Self in us. We must start at the bottom and remain forever at the bottom—mere containers, vessels, capable *only* of receiving, and with no other capability.

Do we see then what this means? Not that we have a life to live with God as our helper. Not that we must pray more, give more, love more, witness more. Not basically that we are God's partners or fellows or co-workers, but that God Himself is the All in us. He is the One who prays, gives, loves, witnesses. He lives our life, our common everyday life—as we shall see more clearly later.

When we have really seen this, then we can add to it the other fact—that we humans are obviously more than inanimate pots and pans. We are people! Humanity has spent all the years of its history running amok with the claim to be autonomous selves, like a horse with the bit between its teeth. Therefore again we say, active self must be thrown right out, as it were, and replaced by receptive self, before we can allow the usurper back into favour again. But if the expulsion has taken place once and for all, and the lesson learned, then the self-in-action can be recognized again in its rightful function, although all our lives it will have to be reminded of where it belongs and snubbed when it tries to take over again. Its rightful place and function is portrayed for us by Christ's parable of the Vine and branch, and Paul's analogy of Head and body. The Vine and branch truth emphasizes the indissoluble union of Christ and the believer. We are organically one. One tree, one life; yet in that relationship Jesus underlined the fact that we, the branches, are merely channels of the sap from the vine. A branch is more than a channel, because a branch is alive whereas a pipe is not, and a branch does absorb and utilize the sap to produce the fruit. It is not entirely inactive, though entirely dependent. But it was the dependence Jesus was pointing to: "apart from Me, ye can do nothing". So that illustration is taking us one further than the vessel. First, we are merely containers. Then, having absorbed and accepted that fact, we are more. We are united to Him whom we contain in a way a vessel can never be united to the liquid in it. We are united because we are living people as He is the Living Person; yet in that union, as branch to vine, we remain as totally dependent as the vessel. Without the sap flowing through us, we can do nothing. Yet it is this time a living dependence, for we are to "abide in the Vine".

Once more then, Paul's illustration takes us further. We are body to head. Again that makes one Person, just as it was one Tree. So one that the Bible even speaks of the body (not the head) as Christ

(1 Cor. 12:12). Yet the body is as solely the agent of the head, as branch of vine. The total dependence is maintained. The union is maintained. But in head and body, the activity of the members comes to the fore. A body is made for action. A head is useless without a body, so the body in Eph. 1:23 is specifically spoken of as the fullness of the head, as the head of the body. They are necessary to each other. So here we come back full circle to active self, but dead, risen and ascended, and thus forever knowing itself as basically containing the Other, motivated by The Other, He living His own life and expressing His own Self through ourselves; yet we freely in action, just as if it was we, thinking, willing, working, laughing, talking, living as normal human beings in normal situations, and the world thinking it is just we, except for something unusual they can't identify about us. What? We know: "your life is hid with Christ in God . . . Christ our life".

But to get all this into focus, we must probe deeper. To recapitulate, God is the one real Person who lives. We live as persons, so that our derived personalities can be the means of manifesting Him. Humanity, as all creation, lives, exists by His life, all are forms of Him; but we being persons, spirits, are the only creatures who can refuse to be what we were made to be—persons who contain The Person. This is what happened, we humans receiving and containing another spirit—the satanic spirit of self-love, the enemy of God. Thus, though we live and move and have our being in Him, we actually live the life that is the exact contrary of His, the life of self-centredness; we express the reverse of God, and are therefore in

His No, not His Yes; in His wrath, not His good pleasure; in His darkness, not His light; in His judgments, not His mercy.

How then can we become that for which we were created? Nothing can function harmoniously, except according to the laws of its being. Humanity in all its history is thus so patently out of gear, right down to each of our personal lives. How can we get into gear?

Chapter Four

Man's Unlearned Lesson

We have already briefly referred to the double fall recorded in the Bible—of Lucifer and of Adam. We have seen what this fall meant—the decisive choice of a created spirit to reject its predestined freedom in the service of God, and to take the road of the unexplored alternative, the possibility of going the opposite way, into the bondage of self-sufficiency, becoming the spirit of self-love in place of containing the Spirit of self-giving. The very name Lucifer, Light-bearer, implies that this exalted being, probably the highest of all created beings according to the descriptions in Isaiah 14:12-15 and Ezekiel 28:11-17, was only to be the manifestor of the Eternal Light, not the light in himself, which no creature can be. He took that "qualitative leap" which broke open the kingdom of hell, of which he became the originator, its god, the father of lies, the primal sinner, the sin-spirit. He set himself to replace God by becoming a god in reverse, and thus "fell" irrevocably, unredeemably from the kingdom of God's heaven, having fixed himself in the total opposite.

The fall of Adam, which has involved us all, was of the same quality, but not the same quantity. There are some significant facts about the account of the fall. Why was Adam set in the garden between two unique trees, both said to be in the midst of the garden, therefore close to each other, both marked out by what is said of them and the names given them as no normal trees? Plainly they were symbolic, for the fruit of no tree gives eternal life or eternal death. Eternal life, we have seen, is a Person, the Spirit of life, and eternal death the same, the spirit of error. These trees represented the two Gods, the Triune God and the god of this world, just as the fruit of a tree still symbolizes Christ our life in the Lord's supper.

What original command, the only command, was given Adam? To eat, for eating is receiving, the basic function of the human self, as we have been continually pointing out. It is most striking that here at the creation of man this was the only command given him, for it is still the only command—"Receive ye the Holy Ghost". "To as many as received Him . . . . " But there was also a prohibition, "Don't eat of the wrong tree". Remarkable that nothing was said to Adam about eating of the right tree, and there was never one indication that he paid any attention to that tree or shewed any interest in it. Why? Because, as intelligent and free people, we must understand who we are and why we are and how we function. These incidents in the Garden of Eden were education, not probation as we are usually told they were. Man must understand himself, then he can act intelligently; which, in its minute way, is the purpose of this small book: to help mixed-up Christians sort things out, starting with themselves. So, in effect, God said to Adam, "Just eat, just learn that is the primary function of a human being—receptivity."

But there was another subtle piece of education wrapped up in this, subtle because man must learn it by himself, and not have it outwardly spoon-fed to him. "Don't eat of the wrong tree" would mean that, as a free being, he could go the wrong way; and supposing he was tempted to do so, then what? There lay the hidden lesson. Humans are containers, to be possessed by another Spirit in the human spirit. They are slaves to be bossed (Rom. 6:16). They do not boss themselves. If therefore Adam feels the pull to go in the wrong direction, it is not in him to resist or refuse. But he and Eve did feel that pull. So then what? There was the tree of life, all the positive power in it to do the right and resist the wrong, for that tree was Christ. Adam never so much as glanced in its direction, because it never dawned on him that humans are basically helpless, and that his deliverance could not be in his own resistance, but only in the counteraction of the Spirit of Truth within him, if he took of Him. He never did. He never even glimpsed the basic lesson man has to learn, and so he was shanghaied straight into the trap. He remained a recipient, for man always is that, but he received the wrong spirit through the wrong tree—"the spirit that now worketh in the children of disobedience", the spirit of self-sufficiency, the spirit of self-love, the spirit of error.

That is why man has to take the long, long trail back to the discovery of his helplessness, a trail that only ends when we reach Romans chapter seven, a trail which has many a booby trap in it, many a tree-root to trip the unwary; and it is a trail nearly always trodden after the new birth, not before, because we have become so completely at home in the illusion of our self-sufficient selves that we do not lightly learn the lesson that the father of our race failed to learn. But we must learn it, because we say again, if God is going to live His life intelligently in intelligent and willing humans, they must learn and accept the truth about themselves as well as about Himself; and that is also precisely why we are busying ourselves about talking these things over in such detail.

Even the facts of the Fall and our consequent condition are rarely known. Few seem to have grasped that man is not just an independent self doing as he pleases and doing it in his own strength. He never has been this. He has always been indwelt by a god. He has always had an inner union—to whom? "Greater is He that is in you (the believer) than *he* that is in the world." Who is this second "he" in the world, if not the Satanic spirit? And he is actually named a few verses later (1 John 4:6): "Hereby know we the Spirit of truth and the spirit of error". We have already quoted the great passage descriptive of the condition of fallen humanity— Ephesians 2:1-3—which includes that statement, "the spirit that now worketh *in* the children of disobedience"; or the other, "*in* whom the god of this world hath blinded the minds . . . ." The fact that is hidden from many is that sin is essentially a person, just as holiness is a Person. Holiness is the "Spirit of holiness" (Rom. 1:4), the Holy Spirit. We have pointed out all along that since the human is the container of the Divine Person, all goodness, love, righteousness, wisdom, power, holiness and the rest are, not we, but HE in us, "Jesus Christ who has been made unto us wisdom, righteousness, sanctification, redemption". But the opposite is equally and logically true. Sin is not a thing, but an indwelling person, the spirit of fear, the spirit of bondage, the evil spirit, the spirit of the world, the spirit of anti-Christ. Sins are that spirit expressing himself through the human faculties and appetites, just as holiness and love are the Other Spirit expressing Himself through the same channels. Thus a pregnant word is spoken of the first sin recorded after the Fall–the sin of Cain, when John says that he "was of that wicked one and slew his brother". Precisely, it was not primarily Cain that was the murderer, but he whom Jesus called "a murderer from the beginning"–through Cain.

This is important because our very premiss is wrong if we think that our first father could have resisted temptation. If he could, we can. But can we? Is not that our problem and failure, until we learn that the way to meet temptation is by recognizing the One in us, and not by struggling against it ourselves? We start mixed-up, if we start by thinking that the Garden of Eden was a scene of probation to try men out. God is no such experimenter, dangling men on a string to see how they will react. God knoweth our frame that we are but dust, and He only puts us through absolutely necessary grades of education that we may learn, even as the Son Himself had to "learn obedience (recognition of His Father in action in Him) through the things which he suffered (temptations)"; and thus we can become eternally free, healthy, happy cooperators with God, knowing exactly who He is and who we are, and loving the relationship.

One other fact should be noted. I said that Adam's fall was qualitatively the same as Lucifer's, but not quantitatively. Lucifer's fall was total. He chose in himself to be a god of another quality, and thus set himself as a rival and alternative to God. His sin and fall were absolute and irrevocable. He became god in reverse. Adam's fall was of the same quality, but not quantity. He fell through the temptation of another, through deceit, lies, misrepresentation. He was responsible and therefore guilty, for he chose to follow instead of seeking the way of escape right there available to him, and therefore his fall had the same quality of disobedience and rebellion; but it was not in quantity complete and absolute in the sense of an open-faced rejection of God. His interest was rather the attractions of the flesh than revolt against God. If he could have kept both God and sin, he would have done so. His outlook was not totally reversed. He had not irrevocably chosen evil to be his good. He was more a kidnapped slave than a willing son of the devil; indeed Scripture speaks of us as children, not sons, of the evil one, and a child is defined as "differing nothing from a servant". Adam, therefore, knew good and evil, whereas Satan knows only evil as his good. Adam had the moral sense, the conscience, the "law written in the heart", an impress of the image of God in him not obliterated as in Satan, and God could and did meet and talk with him immediately after his fall. Adam was redeemable. But more of that and its consequences later.

Chapter Five

God's Problem Solved

Now we can see God's problem, if we may use such human language, and the only possible purpose of redemption. How will He regain for Himself His stolen property—us humans who have become containers and manifestors of that usurping god, the spirit of self-love, in place of Himself, the Spirit of self-giving, whom we had been created to receive in the Tree of life? So often the gospel is preached and the offer of salvation made on a much more superficial level. The idea is given that we are out of step with God through sin, but that a restoration has been made by the atoning death of Christ, which has removed the guilt and eternal consequences of our sins, and restored to us sonship and fellowship with God. Now let us carry on living with the help of God. But, we are then told, we shall not live as we ought to, nor find heart satisfaction unless we own Him as Lord as well as Saviour: Saviour He must be or we are damned: Lord He should be or our lives will be fruitless. To have Him as Saviour is mandatory: to have Him as Lord is optional. What nonsense! Redemption is only redemption when God regains (buys back) for Himself His dwelling place, our human personalities which were created for no other purpose than to contain Him. Therefore unless redemption immediately makes that a fact, and a saved sinner is from that instant the dwelling place of the Living God, there is no salvation.

Through ignorance a redeemed person may not realize what has happened to him and may blunder about as a consequence, but it has happened all the same; and so often the responsibility for our blundering, soulish, flesh-manifesting though redeemed, lives lies at the door of a gospel only half-preached, or believers only half-instructed. And does that not really mean that the preachers themselves are only half-enlightened, because we surely give out what we have within? There is much talk these days of depth-psychology. We surely need evangelical depth-theology. Do we not need to reorientate our gospel message, and tell right out to the non-Christians that we are not bringing them some panacea for happier living or future security? We are bringing them a total revolution, a life which is nothing less than God Himself living in them through the radical replacement effected by Christ crucified and risen, with all the radical consequences which will follow from a Christ-centred in place of self-centred life. And it is by no means merely the non-Christians who need to become Christians. The much harder job is to make the Christians Christians!

God's full salvation! To use human language again, He had two problems to solve; one was His, the other ours. God's problem was broken law. Broken law has inevitable consequences. Law is the term we use to define the way a thing works. It works this way, not that. Break the law and you suffer the consequences. The law of our lungs is that they must have air. Refuse them air and we suffocate. The fundamental law of the universe is love, for God is love. Everything which is not God's self-giving love is broken law; therefore our whole natural life without Christ living in us is broken law, for He only is self-giving love; everything else is self-loving love. The consequence of this broken law is repeatedly made plain in the Bible in terms like everlasting destruction from the presence of the Lord: outer darkness: weeping and gnashing of teeth: indignation and wrath, tribulation and anguish: where the worm dieth not and the fire is not quenched: the lake which burneth with fire forever and ever. How can even God deliver us from such consequences?

The whole Bible revelation from the earliest chapters of Genesis to the end of Revelation gives one plain answer. Substitutionary sacrifice is the only way of "deliverance from the wrath to come", and that sacrifice was the offering of God's own lamb, His Son, whom He "sent to be the propitiation for our sins"; it was actually God Himself "in Christ reconciling the world unto Himself". Such a fact, though attested to by all the centuries of Bible revelation, will forever be an absurdity to natural philosophy. Justification by the blood of Christ—human reason can never take that and never has, nor the other truths concerning Christ coming in the flesh, His incarnation, physical resurrection and return in person; human reason is the vehicle, albeit the highest, of human self-sufficiency; and blinded self never can and never will see God by its own resources. God's truth can only come by God's revelation, not of this world, and is only available to faith; and faith means nothing less than the bowing down and falling prone of proud reason, and the committal of ourselves with all the passion of our being to Someone and Something He did for us which we can never and shall never prove, but do believe. It is the absurdity of faith—to the Greeks in their human wisdom foolishness, and the Greeks live on by their thousands to-day, often in the garb of Christian preachers and seminaries—but to us who believe "Christ, the wisdom of God and the power of God".

By this one tremendous act in history, planned and prepared even before sin and the human race were in existence (which gives us a glimpse into the certainty that God has been managing His own affairs and ours before ever the devil gave the appearance of taking over), what we called God's problem was totally resolved. Not only had the penalty been paid by the One who was made a curse for us; but with that, the guilt was non-existent; forgiveness had become a universal certainty, because the One who forgives is the One who had made the forgiveness possible in His blood; and finality is reached in the term which was such a favourite of Paul's—justification, the condemned criminal leaving the court without a stain on his character, as if he had never committed the crimes. So it is with us who are in Christ by faith—"accepted in the Beloved", "made the righteousness of God in Him". Perfect and forever wonderful.

Chapter Six

Man's Problem Solved

But that has not resolved what we call the second problem—man's problem. Justification removes the consequences of man's sins, but not the source of them. The root must be dealt with, not merely the fruit. If the ultimate problem and cause of all the devastation is the indwelling spirit of error, salvation can only be complete if he is cast out forever, and the union of this false spirit with the human spirit destroyed. If the sole purpose of redemption is that we humans should be God's dwelling place, then it is obvious that a salvation which only removes the guilt and penalty of man's rebellion, but not the rebel king on his usurped throne, has come short of its purpose. God cannot seat Himself on a throne already occupied, nor can He permit a rival claimant within. The New Testament writers, therefore, take us on from the circumference to the centre of Christ's redeeming work, and open to us the inner core of its total accomplishment. It might almost be called the hidden truth; not that it is hidden in the Scriptures, it is presented as plainly and factually as the truth of justification, and is really only a logical extension of it;

but it is hidden in the sense that thousands treasure the outer shell of salvation; far fewer crack the shell and feed on the kernel.

We are entitled to recognize this as a distinct second aspect of the one work of redemption, because Paul presents it as such. Romans 1-5 and 6-8 are the classic passages on the two. In this second one, we are pointed away from a Saviour dying alone on Calvary for our sins, to ourselves who died with Him. We have to look at Christ crucified then from two different points of view. In the first, we see Him dying there alone on our behalf. He trod that winepress alone. He was uniquely our substitute. We gaze on Him there as the Israelites on the brazen serpent, an illustration He Himself used to Nicodemus concerning His coming death. The most sacred word in the Scripture which presents this truth to us is His blood—"the precious blood of Christ, as of a lamb without blemish and without spot". It is a sure sign that a humble believer has divine illumination concerning his sin and Christ's redemption, when that blood is most precious to him and he anticipates worshipping forever at the feet of "the Lamb as it had been slain in the midst of the throne"; and it is equally a danger signal when any who profess to believe, belittle the blood. The blood is the life, as Moses revealed, and His blood was the life of God drained out to its last drop for the whole world.

But then we have a change of emphasis. We no longer look at Christ crucified, and concentrating our attention solely on Him dying for us, see just who He is and what He did for us, and see Him as a lonely figure hanging there. Our attention is now turned to the fact that He did it for *us*. We see Him now as *our* representative. If He was there for us, then *we* were there also. We do not see Him alone now, we rather see ourselves whom He represented. It might be called the reverse side of the one coin. The interest is now centred, not on what He went through to pay the penalty for our sins, but on what effect such a death and resurrection has on us in our present personal lives, in the light of the fact that we went through it with Him. Obviously this is a more difficult mental concept, and that is part of the reason why it is so sidestepped in our thinking, grasping and teaching. Any child can understand the historical fact of the Saviour dying two thousand years ago for us; but it is more difficult to understand a living relationship whereby I myself, a living twentieth century person, actually participated in a scene of 2000 years ago, with certain revolutionary effects on my daily life. But understanding is only one key to a double-locked door. Faith is the other key, and faith is not mental acceptance by human reason, it is passionate inwardness by which our whole being embraces and attaches itself to a Person who just is not to natural reasoning. When that stride of faith has been really taken over the gulf that forever separates natural reason from supernatural revelation, then an inward Christ is met with inwardly ("the Son revealed in me" as Paul wrote of his conversion), and then it is no longer difficult to speak the language or understand the truths of this reverse side of the cross when they are presented to us—we are with Him there.

What then were the consequences of this fact that when He died and rose, it was actually we, the whole world of believers, who died and rose with Him? The fact that He was called by Paul the last Adam is a striking indication. Adam is the progenitor, the forefather of the race. The whole coming race was in his loins as a seed. Therefore what he was, we are. He having received the wrong spirit into him, we are born with that same false indwelling person. As David said, "In sin did my mother conceive me", remembering that sin is basically the spirit of sin, the god of sin. The last Adam, therefore, is God's replacement for the first; indeed in God's perspective and foreordination a negative is always only a type or foreshadowing of its positive, which accounts for Paul saying that Adam was a figure of Him that was to come; and that again is a significant hint to us of what our attitude should be when we pray for needs to be supplied or situations changed. The last Adam is also the progenitor of the last race, to be God's eternal dwelling-place and means of manifestation. God's grace is that He does not create some new race as presumably He could; but He recreates the new out of the old; for love must save, even as we must be co-saviours when Love lives in us. To do this, the last Adam must be born a man among men, and as the God-man in whom Satan had no place, try though he may, go through a death and resurrection. The death would sever the old and false union, the resurrection would be the new union.

I know no three Scriptures which state this more succinctly than 2 Cor. 5:21, Rom. 6:10, 1 Pet. 3:18. The first opens the depth of the Saviour's identification with us. God made Him to be *sin* for us. To bear our sins was to suffer in our stead. To be made sin was to be in God's sight a world indwelt by the spirit of sin. That is the depth to which He went. This in itself was necessary if the next statement was to become fact: "in that He died, He died *unto* sin once". He had died for sins; now it says He died unto sin. When a person dies, body is separated from spirit. When Jesus died, having been made sin (having the spirit of sin), His holy dead body was eternally separated from that sin-spirit; but it was not just Jesus lying there a dead body; it was we. We, all believing people, that moment were cut off from the indwelling usurper. When He arose from the dead, the third statement says He was "quickened by the Spirit", the Holy Spirit of God. Here was the firstborn from the dead of the new humanity with the Spirit of God, His own Spirit united to Him as representing us. We believers were all there also. In Him the old union was forever broken, the new union forever replaced it. God had come into His own.

Here was full salvation, commemorated whenever we partake of the symbols of the body and blood of Christ: the blood by which we are justified and continually cleansed, which was a Christ regarded as dying by Himself for us: the body by which the old union is severed and the new created. Paul, significantly enough, says of those twofold symbols that we are "one bread and one body", for we were identified with Him as His body in His death and resurrection; but he does not say we were one blood, for that was uniquely He Himself.

Chapter Seven

How Acquire Faith?

Now comes the question of experiencing what we may admit to be the truth. How many times I meet this heart cry, "But how make this real to myself? I know it in theory, I believe it mentally, but . . . ." We have to get right down to the fundamental human issue. How do we experience what is beyond experience? How do we know what is beyond knowledge? How do we believe the impossible, unbelievable, absurd? Let us make no mistake about it. Here is where the battle is joined. God's word proclaims an unbridgeable breach in human existence. Man denies this. Man claims that every apparent breach can be bridged on a human level. That claim has been the occupation of philosophy from its beginnings with the Greeks, and the occupation of liberal theology, and the aim of ethics, and the objective of every religion except Christianity, and of a lot of Christianity also. The reason is plain. Admit the breach, and you destroy the autonomy of the self. But self-sufficiency, and a philosophy which will sustain it, is the be-all and end-all of a self-orientated humanity. Therefore sin must be explained away as ignorance or instinct, man's innate goodness must be postulated, and man's way to God smoothed through a supposed faith in our innate rootage in Him, or in His supposed character of undiscriminating love; or in the acceptability of our repentances, contrition, religious observances and so forth. Anything that preserves the integrity of the self and provides some mediation with the Eternal of which human reason and dignity can approve.

But sin, creating an unbridgeable gulf between ourselves and God! What is that? Human reason can neither stomach nor explain that. And a movement over from the Other Side, of the Eternal into time, of the Invisible and Unknowable into a human body, of the Absolute into a relative existence, of the Creator among the created! Such is the outside limit of absurdity! So we come right up against it. Is faith easy? Yes, when you have got accustomed to it—at least easier. No, when the first trembling steps are being taken. Faith means something far more than repeating a creed. It means something that has penetrated us on the inside. It is not just truth in general. It is *my* truth. Not just the gospel, but *my* gospel. In other words something has stirred within which has been dawning light to us, not of ourselves. It has come from the Other Side. The Bible word is conviction—of the Spirit. Some word from God has reached us which we just *know* to be true. In my own case, it was when, as a lad of eighteen, my football ambitions were shattered by an accident, and in hospital just one thought crossed my mind. Is there nothing but selfishness in the world? For I am totally selfish: my father, my mother, my home, the world is for me! I could not then have said that was the Spirit of God. But I knew it was truth. I would not even have recognized it as a flash from the Other Side. But it was. It was the *preparatio evangelica* for me. It conditioned me to recognize myself, not just as one that thought and did things of which I was ashamed, but as a sinner before the Ultimate, before God. That again was revelation: the sudden recognition that God is holy, I unholy, and therefore eternally unfit to dwell with Him. And finally the flash of thought into my mind that Jesus Christ, God's Son, really did shed His blood for me, and therefore there was not wrath, but acceptance for me. Could I prove one of those things? Not one. Could I be sure that it was God who said them to me, introduced them into my thinking? No. Teaching had something to do with it. I had been taught through the years the Bible and the gospel. But external teaching does not save. It may be fuel for the lamp of the Spirit, that is all. How does God speak then, and how do we believe? I don't know, because it all comes from the Other Side.

That precisely is faith. The nearest we can say is that through the human faculties of mind and heart there come to all (I believe) hidden communications of the Spirit, disturbances of the status quo, of our rationalizations, our funk holes in which we try to hide our sinfulness from ourselves and from Him, our false pursuit of satisfaction in things of time and sense, our build-up of a human ethic, religion, philosophy or idealism which crumbles when matched with the actual realities of our self-centred lives, or our pretended and endeavoured forms of communion with God. As we respond to these pricks, which was the name given to the goadings of the Spirit in the apostle Paul, further revelations of inner truth come to us, revelations to us if to no one else, revelations which have their ultimate source and guarantee in the

Scriptures: "if they speak not according to this word, there is no light in them".

But the moment comes when we settle it, or rather God settles it in us. We can prove nothing. The wise of this world may be able to shoot holes in our logic or reasons. We readily grant that the One in whom we now have put our faith is unknowable to the world, invisible, and we can never say we know or see Him except by faith. Historic facts are available, but again we admit that history is unprovable. We have only the word of the historians or eyewitnesses. We have no ultimate grounds upon which to base our belief in the reliability and infallibility of the Bible; indeed plenty can be brought against it. We further admit that certain facts concerning the life and death of Christ are altogether beyond human probabilities—His deity, His incarnation, His physical resurrection, His ascension. Pile question mark upon question mark, we admit all. But faith has nothing to do with these. Faith is itself from the Other Side, and is as inexplicable and absurd as that in which it believes. Faith has nothing to say for itself beyond the bare statement that from certain inward convictions which are convictions to it, it stakes its all on God as truth in His revelation through the Bible and supremely the Christ of the Bible. For myself I have stated the two main convictions which constrained me forty-seven years ago to gamble my life on God: first, what was the obvious, that I was a 100 per cent self-centred person; and second, that God was the wholly opposite, 100 per cent self-giving, so that He actually gave Himself in the Person of His Son to change me into His likeness. That final fact convinced me. I said I could follow to eternity a God who is forever the

Servant of His own creation, even to the point of giving His own life for His enemies; and I could wish for nothing higher than that such a Person could and should live that same quality of life through selfish me. And so say I to-day.

Faith is built on doubt. Doubt is its lifeblood. Don't let us be mistaken about that. Faith is doubt absorbed, doubt conquered. Unbelief (unfaith) is doubt accepted. Unbelief is an act of will as much as faith. Doubt is not an act of will, but is the only attitude we humans can have towards anything external to us until we decide whether to accept it or reject it. The uncertainty, the doubt, is the very element which gives stimulus and passion to the decision. Faith then is built on doubt. As the philosopher Immanuel Kant says in his *Critique of Pure Reason*, "Nothing which is intuited in space is a thing-in-itself.... What we call outward objects are nothing else but mere representations of our sensibility, whose real cor-related thing-in-itself is not known by means of these representations, nor ever can be.... The things which we intuit are not in themselves the same as our representation of them in intuition.... What may be the nature of objects considered as things-in-themselves and without reference to the receptivity of our sensibility is quite unknown to us."

Every smallest action is conquered doubt. You eat food. How do you know it won't poison you? You sit on a chair. How do you know it won't collapse under you? You go to visit a certain home. How do you know it will be there when you get there? Action, therefore, on every level is conquered uncertainty. You make up your mind that there is every possible likelihood that a thing is what it appears to be and will react as you expect it to, and then you act—by faith. The more uncertainty there is, the more passion in your decision of faith, for there has been a bigger doubt to conquer. Should you or should you not marry that person? Should you move over there and accept that new job? Should you invest in that company?

But at least your eyes and ears and perhaps your friends are there to encourage you in your acts of faith. Such actions are usually accepted as normal or sensible. But when you move over to faith in God! There is these days in our so-called Christian countries even a respectable Christian faith. It is the done thing to be a church member. You were probably baptized into the church as an infant. It probably does not cost you more concern to be an adherent of the Christian faith than it does to choose your clothes, for it really is the same quality of faith in the visible, faith in your church's outward creed. But this is not the saving inward faith of which we are speaking. This faith costs everything, because it means taking seriously what cannot be taken halfheartedly, the challenge of an invisible Person who comes to claim His ownership of you, and offers you no proof beyond what inner convictions He gives you through His word, and even that cannot be proved by outward proofs to be His word. You are called to be a fool of faith, you are called to believe what this time does not carry with it at least a measure of common sense and obvious likelihood, but "entereth into that within the veil whither the forerunner is for us entered, even Jesus". If a faith must have some inward passion and conviction in it which will motivate a man to make some crucial earthly decision, how much more conviction and passion must be in a faith which has no earthly sanctions, yet will reorientate the whole of life.

Now then again we ask the question, What will make meaningful to me these tremendous truths of Christ living His life in me, and I united to Him in place of the old union? The answer, of course, is faith. But that doesn't seem to act. I do believe, and yet it seems to make little difference. Well, there is still no other answer. But it is possible that you are not really believing in God's impossible word. You think you are, but you are really believing in what you think about that word. I told you that it costs everything to believe. "Let us labour therefore . . . lest any man fall after the same example of unbelief". Faith crosses an unbridgeable gulf into the invisible, unknowable, impossible. It crosses just by believing it has crossed, because He says so, and He is the bridge. To everything on the human side of the gulf it looks as unbridgeable as ever, and that there is no other side! If therefore, without realizing it, you are basing your faith on a single personal reaction to your faith, then you are still on the human side of the gulf. You are really believing in yourself, not in Him who takes you to the Other Side. A man said to me, "Please help me, I feel a barrier between myself and Christ". I investigated and found that he had faith in an indwelling Christ, and had no barrier of immediate uncleansed sin; so I said, "You are wasting your time asking for help from an illusion. There is no barrier except that you have transferred your faith back from Him to yourself—what you feel about your relationship to Him. Get back where you were—to faith without a shred of human assistance." Another said the same to me about power. How could he know the power of God? "Does Jesus Christ dwell in you?" I asked. "Yes," he said— "by faith." "Then run away," I said (he was a young man). "What more power can you want or have than He in you? You are wanting to exchange faith for sight. Faith has no other evidence than itself (he that *believeth* hath the witness in himself). You have turned back to find some missing evidence by believing what you feel in place of what He is." Yet a third asked, "How can I know He abides in me?" Rather brutally I answered, "I am not the least interested in whether you know or do not know. I am only interested in whether He is in you or not. What you know directs your faith on to what you know, not what He is."

On the human side of the gulf we humans want all our human proofs of feelings, evidences, results and so forth. On the other side of the gulf, and the bridge over the gulf, is the One who is forever unknowable and invisible to the human; and faith has staked all on Him, indeed the faith itself is really only He in us believing in Himself—there's nothing human left to it. If I hold a book in my hand and say, "This is a book", I am only directing your and my own attention to the fact of the book. That is faith in the fact that the book is a book. If I say to you, "I believe this is a book", I am diverting your and my attention from the fact of the book being a book to my views and beliefs about the book. I have transferred your potential faith from the book to myself and my opinions. That is what we are continually doing, and is the cause of much weakness and wavering in faith.

I think that part of our spiritual education at the hands of God has necessarily to be dry times, times when He appears to have withdrawn His presence, times when the Bible ceases to speak to us, prayer is dull, our heart seems cold, fruit seems to be nil; and such times are most healthy for us till we have thoroughly learned this one lesson—the difference between faith which has gone onto the Other Side because it has merely been His own believing in Himself in us, and we have nothing more to do with it than just to relax in the fact that He is believing in Himself in us; the difference between such a faith of God and *our* faith which is composed of how I feel about Him, how I know or don't know Him, how I see or don't see Him at work, and so on. When we have learned the difference, we walk as naturally and composedly in dark as in light, in dry as in fruitful times, because it is nothing to do with us; the faith, being God's faith, is impervious to the storms that blow in the visible world. To a large extent, the variations disappear between dry and fresh, dull and bright, hot and cold, fruitful and fruitless, shewing that they were largely psychological and illusory to a faith that is fixed.

So we come down to this. Certain facts are presented to us through the revelation of God's word. The birth of faith is the inward conviction that these are the truth for me. Therefore I receive and believe them, and in doing so transcend all natural doubts either about the truth of them or their efficacy in my own life. I transcend the doubts by replacing them by deliberate faith; actually their opposition is what gives sinews to my faith. The subtlest form of doubt will be psychological, the questioning in my own mind whether these things are really so, because I don't feel or see their effect on me, because they still appear unreal to me, and so on. But I learn by these very pressures that what has appeared at first to be my faith in these facts was in reality a faith imparted to me, God's faith, without which I should never have been able to perceive or receive these facts as facts; therefore I relax in the midst of such doubts and questionings, not trying to believe, but affirming that it has been taken out of my hands. God has done the believing in me; then leave Him to it, for the facts are that He Himself now lives His own life in me.

But supposing I say that I am not sure whether I am willing to face the implications of Christ living in me. There are things in my life I would not be willing for Him to take from me or tell me to do; there are things I would find it impossible to change, or do not want to change, habits, or attitudes or practices; there are confessions I might have to make, people I might have to forgive or love, whom I do not love. Self cannot change self. God is not asking that unwilling self become willing self, because it cannot. God asks nothing from us, because there is nothing we can give or do. We go right back to our foundations; humans are capable of receiving, not doing. Being intelligent and free, there is only one requirement—that we just honestly admit ourselves to be what we are: if unwilling, say so; if fearful that things might be required of us which we couldn't do, say so; if we have habits we can't break, or relationships or attitudes we don't know how we could change or even want to, say so; then, having been honest as far as we know how, it is "over to Him", we simply dare to affirm that He is what He is in us by grace, or becomes so at this moment, and dare to believe that He will change what needs changing. It is nothing to do with what we see or feel about it; faith is not in our reactions, but in Him and His word as fact.

In doing that, in affirming a God-implanted faith in this tremendous fact of Christ's full redemptive work in us, replacing the spirit of self-love in us by His Spirit of self-giving, implicit in such a faith is the recognition that He is going to live another quality of life in us, and that therefore He will make any necessary changes in us, even though humanly we are not even willing. He will impart His willingness to us, which will not only overcome our unwillingness, but actually change us into willing His will with Him, according to Paul's statement that "it is God which worketh in us to will and to do of His good pleasure"; and note that it is His good pleasure, and if He enjoys what He does in us, we shall enjoy it too.

I know no better account of the reality of the struggle of a self confronted with the offer of God to live in that life, wanting it yet not wanting it, facing its implications pragmatically point by point, than the chapter in the life of *Rees Howells, Intercessor*[1] on how he received the Holy Ghost; how ultimately he had to come to the crisis point, and cried out he was not willing, but the Voice came back to him, Are you willing to be *made* willing? And that ended the week-long conflict.

But again we ask, because it is often asked, Does the committal of faith mean that we have an inner witness to our believing? There are those indeed who urge people to "hold on", "wait", "pray through" until they do, and say that they cannot be truly sure that they have received what they have asked for, until they have that witness. It is not for us to decry any

---

[1] *Rees Howells, Intercesor;* Lutterworth Press.

approach of a seeking soul to God, and certainly not an approach which has brought deliverance and the certainty of the Holy Spirit to thousands. God is so much bigger than our puny understanding, and meets us on the level of our heart's desire. Let each pursue and advocate the way God has made real to us. There is a witness of the Spirit, the Bible is plain on that. "He that believeth on the Son of God hath the witness in himself" was a key text in the early Methodist revivals, and is in the foreground of the teaching of most "Holiness" bodies, and the Pentecostals, and the Salvation Army. But I cannot say that it is given the place of importance in the Scriptures. Everything there is the one word—faith. Implicit in faith is that it brings its own witness; but that is secondary, and remarked on incidentally. The obvious danger of regarding the witness as the necessary evidence of faith is that it brings us back once again to gauging faith by feelings. To make the witness the sign of faith is that same retrogression from simply seeing Him who is invisible by the nakedness of faith, which truly honours Him and His unchanging word, to needing some boost to faith, which is really believing in what we feel of Him, and not unconditionally in Him.

The Scriptures do not speak of the witness as a sign, but merely as the inevitable outcome of living faith. When we believe, we have the witness, because faith is its own witness. Therefore the witness is not experienced by seeking it, but by occupation in believing, and believing is just constantly recognizing Christ within—by faith. And if we do not "feel" a witness? Well, keep on believing, even if we die without a witness. It is the old, old snare. Where can I find joy? Where peace? Where power? By seeking *them*, which really means seeking *my* feelings of joy, peace, power? No. By seeing *Him*—by faith. HE is the joy, peace, power, all. He *is* that whether we feel it or not. Keep occupied in affirming Him by faith, even though I feel as heavy as lead or as weak as water, or as disturbed as a windstorm. Keep believing Him *in* these conditions. Whether and when they change is His business. If we have Him, we have all. We shall and do experience Him as all these; but I am almost afraid to say that, because we then turn back again and say, "Well, where are they? I don't feel them." And we are back again on the self-level. It is safer to say that I have only Him as my all. How He manifests Himself is entirely His business, and His way is perfect. If I never have a witness of Him (and I have known saints of God who have lived and died practically with no inner witness), we still have Him; and maybe I shall find one day that the *trial* of my faith (not my faith, but its trial—having to walk with God in the dark maybe) has been, as Peter said, more precious than gold that perisheth, and will be found peculiarly "unto praise and honour and glory at the appearing of Jesus Christ".

A friend going through a dark patch was deeply disturbed lest he had lost his salvation. "Well," I said, "what matter anyhow? It is not a thing called salvation you have received, but a Person. Let Him walk in you where He pleases. If He wants to walk in you in hell, leave that to Him." And then I told him what my father-in-law, C.T. Studd, had said when I was with him in Africa, and a violent critic had written questioning whether Studd really knew the Lord at all or had a devil. "Well," said Studd, "if I have a devil, I shall go to hell. But if I go there, I shall get so busy preaching the gospel to the devils, that Satan will open the doors quick and put me outside before I steal all his people for Jesus!" So the point is, just keep walking with Jesus—by faith, and let everything else fit in as it may.

Another question, tossed like a ball from one to the other, is whether what we have been writing about is specifically a "second experience" in the life of a believer. Is it a "second work" of grace quite distinct from regeneration? Is it something farther on than justification? Is there still some specific deposit of sin, or old nature, or flesh remaining in the believer which has to be dealt with or removed by this second step of faith?

Chapter Eight

The Second Work of Grace?

Once again I think I should be very foolish and presumptuous if I sought to be an iconoclast and wipe out at a sweep what I might consider not to be the exact balance of truth, as if wisdom would die with me. I am deeply convinced that within the limits of a few fundamentals concerning God's dealings with man through Christ, there is latitude for many varieties of emphasis and interpretation. I think the proof of that is the variety in the church of Christ, tens of thousands finding and loving and serving Him, yet many with doctrinal teachings on nonessentials which others may call mistaken or erroneous. Has not God got thousands of His redeemed people in the Anglican or Episcopal church, and in the Presbyterian, Lutheran, Baptist, Methodist? And what about those queer people who are called fringe sects by their more respectable brethren who were themselves the despised sects of a few generations ago? The Brethren, the Bible churches, the Interdenominationals (of whom I am one), the Holiness, the Pentecostals? Are not many of us in Christ also? Are there not God's saints among the Roman Catholics, despite what is to us the overload of unscriptural dogmas?

With that in mind, then, we return to this question of the "second work of grace". I can only share what I see. I do not believe that the Scripture teaches such as a necessity on the basis that there was something left undone at regeneration which still has to be done in the believer. A devastating examination of this, a book doubtless which will be anathema to any ardent "second-work-of-grace-ers", is Benjamin W. Warfield's *Perfectionism*. I think Warfield is far too far out on a limb in his total lack of sympathy or appreciation of what God has done through "Victorious life" teaching. I cannot in the least go with him in this; but I suppose a good controversialist is always black or white; and he does convincingly undercut a lot of loose teaching on sanctification.

The position, as I see it, is that there is only one work of salvation, completed by one Saviour in one death, resurrection, ascension and one coming of the Holy Spirit. All that had to be done was then done. When we receive Him, we receive Him in all the completeness of His Saviourhood, which by the Holy Ghost takes practical effect in us. We are justified by his blood, we are cut off from the old indweller who is replaced by the new Indweller (dead, buried and risen with Him). We walk in newness of life.

But very few new converts understand what the new life really is into which they have entered. Even if we have a mental understanding, we are not yet conditioned in experience to realize the depths of the meaning of the Christ-life replacing the self-life. In general we have not seen beyond the wonder of sins forgiven, and our adoption through grace into the family of God, and the way of access open to us to "find grace to help in time of need". We therefore thresh about like a fish in shallow water, and our lives seem to be more self-effort and flesh-manifestation than a walk in the Spirit. Now if our interpretation of the new life in Christ is faulty, we may have mistaken ideas about there being some entity still in us, some nature or flesh or something which was not removed at the new birth, but must be removed by a definite further work of the Spirit; and there seems lots about us that looks like it!

But let us get our facts straight. We humans, as we have seen, have always been containers of another, the false god or the True. The nature we have manifested has not been our own; it has been the nature of the one indwelling us. These are the two natures the Bible speaks of. In our unredeemed condition we were "by nature the children of wrath", because we contained the "spirit that now worketh in the children of disobedience". In our redeemed lives, there have been given to us "exceeding great and precious promises, that by these ye might become partakers of the divine nature". We were "slaves of sin", now we have become "slaves of righteousness". In the old the trend of our lives was downward on the road of self-love. In the new the trend of our lives is upward on the road of self-giving. This is what the Bible means by the old man and new man. The old man was I with the old spirit within me, the new man is the same I with the new Spirit within me. We can never be old man and new man at the same time, for the one becomes the other. "Seeing that ye have put off the old man with his deeds; and have put on the new man": not put one on top of the other, like an overcoat over a coat, but taking off one to wear the other.

Have we got that clear, because many have not? We, the human we, appetites and faculties, remain unchanged. We are the agents, responsible agents certainly, willingly involved with our bosses in their activities, but still only the agents. It is the boss who is changed. So we the humans remain the same in old man and new man. It is the boss who changes. So Paul says, "Reckon yourselves to be dead indeed unto sin . . . yield yourselves unto God as those that are alive from the dead"—the same human selves in each case. Nor must we think that the change from the one to the other is seasonable or variable, this way to-day, that to-morrow. No, this is the exchange of the ages for us. Once for all, by the committal of faith, we have seen and affirmed the fact that we died with Christ, which was once for all the end of us as the old man with the old spirit in us; and once for all we have risen with Him and become the new man with the new Spirit in us. "In that He died, He died unto sin *once*, but in that He liveth, He liveth unto God. *Likewise* (once for all) reckon ye yourselves dead . . . alive . . . ." We die daily, that is in another context altogether which we shall refer to later; but we were crucified and risen once and never to be repeated. I hope we have that clear.

Why then do we still commit sins if we are this new man in Christ? What is it in us that sins? A sensible question. I will counter it by another. If the new man sometimes does bad things, how does the old man sometimes do good things? For he does. For an answer we go back to the name given to the forbidden tree in the Garden—the tree of the knowledge of good and evil. We might have thought that if the one was the tree of life, the other would be the tree of death; if the one was plain good, the other would be plain evil; but it was a mixture of the two, which is the condition of the world to-day. Good is predominant; if it were not, nature could not survive, nor peoples. We have explained why it is that we know what we should be with the work of the law written in our hearts, why mankind constantly talks of the ideals it cannot reach: there should be world brotherhood, there should be share and share alike, there should be honesty, integrity, unselfishness. We never reach these because they are not our nature, but merely external influences upon us. Our unredeemed nature is the indwelling spirit of self-love. That is the direction in which we are going. Upward influences have merely a temporary effect on us and we give temporary response, but they are not the real we. Most of us in our unregenerate days felt those influences upon us, religion, ethics, social concerns for the underprivileged, "good works". Most of us participated to some extent—but it wasn't the real we. There was a distinct difference between our nature and the influence upon us. In our ignorance of our true condition we probably thought that we were partly good and partly bad, and others, who equally had not seen into the roots of the human situation, may have thought the same. Good people, splendid people, grand people, fine people, that's how the people of the world are usually busy complimenting each other—till one crosses the path of the other in some unpleasant way. Then the tune changes, because self-love is our basic nature, and we revert to type.

The infinite qualitative difference between human love at its highest and divine love is given us in Rom. 5:6-10. Human love can even give its life for a cause or person it approves, "peradventure for a good man some would dare to die." But human love still has self at the centre, and it cannot give itself for those who hurt it. That is solely the quality of divine love. Christ died for the helpless who couldn't give a thing in return: for sinners who defied and despised Him: for enemies who would murder Him if they got a chance, and who did. That is God's love.

In other words our nature is one thing, influences upon our nature another. In our unredeemed condition, the influences to which we temporarily responded were upward, we were tempted upward; but such responses did not make us good, because we were owned by the evil (self-loving) spirit. We continued basically to walk that same broad road to destruction.

It is equally so in the redeemed life. We need to get one fact clarified. We must not locate either evil or good fundamentally in us humans. Evil is a person, good is a Person. Evil is that spirit of evil, good the Holy Spirit. That is why when Jesus as a man was called "Good Master", He immediately repudiated the name and said, "Why callest thou Me good? There is none good but one, that is, God." And when Peter on one occasion urged Him to look to His own self-preservation, Jesus said to him, "Get thee behind Me, Satan: for thou savourest not the things that be of God, but those that be of men." Jesus traced a self-interested statement back through Peter to its source in Satan. He did not mean that Peter was permanently possessed by Satan. He had just told Peter that he had the Spirit of God (Matt. 16:17); but Peter was responding to a temporary influence downward. Just as the good was not in Jesus as the Son of man, nor the evil in Peter, so with us.

Our nature is the nature of the one who indwells us, and we share that nature and live that quality of life. Being free humans, we share responsibility also, and the consequences; but the prime mover, the real source, is not we but he or He. So in the redeemed life. Now the nature is upward, but the influences downward; but they are only influences, not nature. Just as the good deeds in our unredeemed life were temporary responses, and not the life of the real us; so the sins we commit in the redeemed life are temporary responses, and not the real we. The proof, of course, is that when we commit them, we regret it. We return in spirit to Him to whom we belong, who is our new nature within. His seed remains in us, we *cannot* sin in the sense of giving ourselves to it, plunging into it, loving it, because we are born of God. We are certainly and often overtaken in faults, but they are responses to the influences of this mixed world.

An illustration I sometimes use, based on John Bunyan's *Holy War*, is to think of the human personality as a medieval castle. A castle has a lord over it. The former lord was Satan. We have opened the gates to the conqueror, Jesus Christ, and He has evicted the former lord and taken over. Now Satan is outside, but says to himself, "If I cannot own the castle, I at least will try and bluff them into thinking I do." So when the sentinels on the walls are not as vigilant as they should be, he slips two of his soldiers over (two sins). Once inside, they display Satan's

The Second Work of Grace?

banner and shout out, "We own this castle." What a lie! Two invading soldiers don't own a castle. Throw them out again!

Chapter Nine

A Crisis in Most Lives

We are now just about ready to answer the question, Is there a second work of grace in the believer? We have seen that at the moment of faith a new union became an eternal actuality, and an old union eternally dissolved; but that, because our eyes are dim, few of us at the time of regeneration really know what has happened, or are in a condition to grasp it. In the main we have seen as far as God's wrath on us as sinners, and His mercy on us through Christ, and His acceptance of us in Him. That the old man has become the new man: that the new man is Christ in me: that the big I is in the little i to the point that He is the real I, and my little human i His means of self-expression—that is probably beyond me. Often a period of struggle and failure has to intervene, because, not really knowing in heart experience the "not I, but Christ" life, I battle on as best I may, carrying my burdens, trying to serve Him, living in strain, finding my efforts at maintaining my spiritual equilibrium very futile. I do not even see that it is really I, my little redeemed I, running my own life.

The Bible is full of such examples, in fact nearly all whose biographies are given in any detail are shewn going through their "wilderness" period, when all their real troubles are not the situations they are in, but their futile efforts at handling those situations themselves—not knowingly or deliberately going at it the wrong way, but in sheer ignorance. They just don't see what their true condition is. Jacob is a famous example, not at all because he was deceitful (the sin of his father Isaac was much more reprehensible), but because his urgent questing self on stretch for God's promised inheritance was his own chief stumbling block, until at last God caught him and broke him at Peniel. But so also Moses, Joshua, David, and all the list of them through to Peter and the apostles, and right on up to ourselves.

In this sense, then, there is for most of us a second work of grace, if we like to call it that. There is a day, a season, usually prefaced by many agonizing days, when at last our straining self, stretched and taut like an elastic, gives way. We were crucified with Christ all along, but now faith enters into this intelligently as fact. If we were crucified with Him, we also rose with Him, and now at last we can see that that means the New One within is living His life in us. He always was since redemption, but He had to spend those months and often years working us out of ourselves by walking in us into all sorts of frustrating situations, which we handled wrongly every time by our self-reactions to them; and I reckon the Indwelling Christ has many a laugh as He sees us bumbling and stumbling along, and knows the good though painful lessons we are learning by stubbing our toes on this and then that; but knowing also that we shall see, because He has already started looking out on things His way through our eyes, and will go on until we learn and accept the difference between us looking through our own eyes and He looking through them.

This is a crisis in many lives. It was in mine; and with the example of most of the men and women of the Bible, we are surely justified in saying that it is a necessary crisis in most of our lives. The two days of my life were when I first found Christ (really He found me), and when, in a forest village in the heart of Africa, I at last came to the crisis point of accepting as fact in myself the two truths of Galatians 2:20—the negative and positive: that I had been crucified with Him, and that He was now the real I in me: and I did it in faith without a trace of emotional response; nor did I have anything of that nature for two years after; and my faith is not now fixed on that inner assurance two years later, but on the fact of Galatians 2:20.

The cross has to be real before there can be a steady realization of the resurrection. It is a real death in experience, and probably there has to be a period when we are much more conscious of our having died with Him than having risen with Him. By no other means can we be understanding servants of Christ. We must have really tasted of the self-defeating activities of independent self in our redeemed lives, and have really become soured on them. We must have come to some final point of desperation and despair to have learned our lesson with an utter finality that this way of life, of us serving Christ rather than of Him serving Himself in and by us, is a spill-over into our new lives of the great curse of the Fall, the delusion of self-sufficiency. It has to be a revelation—that the ultimate form of sin is a misuse of self, just as it then can become a personal revelation that the misuse of self is what was removed in the cross and is thus removed in us. And then can come the revelation of Christ, the real new Self in ourselves.

My conclusion, therefore, is that we have not a right to preach and stress the necessity of a "second work of grace" on the grounds that there is an old nature still left in the believer, which was not removed at regeneration, and has to be removed by this additional work of the Holy Spirit. If it is put like that, then the implication is that for some unexplained reason the fullness of salvation through grace is not available to any simple believer by the one act of saving faith. There is something mysteriously held back in the application of the full effects of Christ's completed work which was consummated at Pentecost. And if this is so, then of course a "second blessing" is a *sine qua non* for all. But it is plain to me that the New Testament presents us with all in Christ, with no arbitrary subdivisions in stages of experience. Two passages which make that plain are the way Paul equates sanctification with justification, when in Rom. 6:3 he asks the believers if they do not already know that the symbol of baptism included both; and when in Gal. 2:16-20 he writes of justification by Christ and crucifixion with Christ as part of the same faith-inheritance.

But when it comes down to the pragmatic question, Have I experienced Christ's full salvation, that is a different matter. I may come short through ignorance or through not yet being conditioned to understand the depths of my need and therefore the fullness of His supply. I may need and have a second crisis of faith, as most of us do, not because I have only received a partial salvation, but because the fullness of Christ in me and the fullness of what He has delivered me from, has not been recognized and utilized by me. It is not that something more has to happen in me which has not yet happened, but that I, in my ignorance, act as though something has not happened which has happened. When I have $50,000 in the bank, but by mistake think it is $5000, I live on the $5000 level. When I discover my mistake, I cash a second cheque—the second blessing!

It may seem a hair-split for one to say, "You haven't got. You ought to have. Get it!" And the other, "You have got. You just didn't know it. Use it!" But it does affect the attitude of the recipient. In the former case, he seeks and asks and has to make certain he obtains, and looks for proofs that he has obtained. That may be hard work, and there might be uncertainty at the end of it. In the latter case, he has nothing to do but to reckon on what is already his, be thankful, and go ahead using it—by faith.

Chapter Ten

Signs—With or Without?

Those who say that there is something not yet done in the believer which must be done, or not yet given which must be given, will also attribute the delay to lack of faith. But what they really mean is that faith must produce an evidence, that somehow or other God must give something which the believer can know is His word or sign to them. I think the issue is joined there. God does give signs, these are evident in the history of the early church; but signs are not faith, they are subsequent to faith. They are not even the accompaniment of faith which, if they were, would at once turn faith into sight, and thus annul faith. They are the trimmings of grace; but the joint is the joint without them. All the great saints of the ages, who have endured as seeing Him who is invisible, bear witness that signs and outward manifestations are the toys of childhood compared to the "naked vision"— "the flight of the alone to the Alone".

If I say that there is a hold-back in the Donor, which means that He Himself in His completeness is not yet my All in all, because there is something He has first to do in me which will somehow change me and fit me to contain Him, and that He summons me to faith that He will do this, then that takes me in my faith off *Himself* on to what He will do in *me*. I then have to agonize and seek and tarry until I have evidence that He has done it in *me*. To faith in Him in me must be added witness to something done in myself. This I think is where we part company. To me the gospel is Christ in me—period. He replaces the false spirit in me. The human self of me—spirit, soul, body—does not change, for good or evil are not primarily located in me, I am only a slave to Him who is the goodness, as formerly I was slave to him who is the evil. Therefore there is not some *thing* further to be done in *me* after regeneration. The gospel is "the Son revealed in me", "Christ liveth in me", Christ "mighty in me towards the Gentiles"—Paul's threefold testimony in his letter to the Galatians. Faith is in this fact of "Christ in you the hope of glory".

Faith may have to take a fresh stride forward in appreciation of the fuller meaning of that fact and it may be reasonable and right to call that the "second work of grace", when it refers specifically to the truth of our dying and rising *with* Christ, whereas up till then His dying *for* us had been all we had really appropriated. As we have pointed out, that has to come as the reality to most of us subsequent to the new birth, and I do not believe such a profound crisis of faith can be simply palmed off ironically by saying, "Second blessing? Yes, and then the third and fourth and fifth." For most of us, it has not been just one of a thousand further blessings; but one as distinct as the first supreme moment of rebirth.

So, Second work of grace? Second blessing? Yes, if we safeguard the statement by explaining that we do not mean something further that has to be done to and in us as saved sinners which was not done at regeneration. We affirm that in receiving Christ we received the All in all, for the gospel is not a change in the container, but a change of the Person whom we contain, and the only change in us is the quality of life manifested by us as a consequence (a mighty change!). But because we are usually too blind at our new birth to grasp inwardly what has happened to us, we stumble about in confusion and frustration; and that is God's way of educating us, until we can see more clearly the illusion of self-sufficiency which we have carried over from our old life, and are ready for the profounder affirmation of faith that Galatians 2:20 and Romans 6:1-13 are also facts in us. If we call that the second work of grace, alright.

But in speaking of the self-exposure God has to give us, as He did to Moses, Jacob, Job, Peter, and the rest, to condition us for the revelation of Christ as the Other Self in us, I do not mean that it must always precede faith. When there is sufficient understanding to take the stand of faith that He is Himself in us, we take it. Much will depend on the level of teaching we have. To refrain from such a faith until we feel that something has happened to fit us for it would be moving right back from faith to works. "Received ye the Spirit by the works of the law or by the hearing of faith?" (only hearing, not experiencing anything). "Are ye so foolish? Having begun in the Spirit, are ye now made perfect by the flesh?" Many seem stumbled, as we have already pointed out, by a sense that they believe mentally, but not yet in the depths of their heart. We must not be stumbled by that. To hear intelligently is itself an evidence of an opened ear, which means an opened heart behind the ear. No, let us be thankful if it is given us to apprehend by any of our faculties that this wonderful Christ-in-you relationship is a fact. While we go on believing up to the measure of faith given us, God will go on working the consciousness of the fact in us, until we can cry with the Psalmist, "O God, my heart is fixed, my heart is fixed". Making Himself real to us in experience is God's business. Believing Him, quite apart from experience, is our business.

Some will raise the question of the gifts of the Spirit, or "the baptism of the Spirit", and whether they should be in operation in all our lives. Is the baptism of the Spirit a special impartation of the Spirit subsequent to conversion? Is the initial evidence of this baptism speaking in tongues? Have none of us been "baptized" or filled with the Spirit unless we have had this sign? Is such an experience something beyond what we have just been thinking about in the Christ-in-you relationship?

Again the answer must be inclusive to embrace the plain evidence of the Spirit in the body of Christ. To say that He does not give those gifts in our day, particularly the most unusual and startling of them, the gift of tongues, is to hide our heads in the sand. Tens of thousands of godly, Christ-loving people speak with tongues. Are they all deluded or fleshly or devil-possessed? I don't believe any fair investigator could say so. What is more, whereas up till very recently this gift, together with the gift of healing, was largely confined to the section of God's people we call Pentecostals, to-day these gifts are making their appearance in the older denominations; and while the majority of evangelicals look askance at them and often refuse to have those with the gift of tongues in their ranks, the so-called more liberal wing of the church is evincing marked interest, and calling on their people to face the challenge of the greater zeal and rapid increase of their brother Pentecostals.

Yet there is equal evidence, the evidence of the centuries, that the Spirit of God has been as mightily upon hundreds of thousands of His people who have never had this gift. There is to my mind also plain evidence from the Scriptures that the writers who were expounding the faith in their epistles had no special concern for the manifestation of that gift, nor indeed a great deal to say about any of the twenty specified gifts of the Spirit, except to remark that all believers were privileged with some gift of the Spirit or another, as He divides to "every man severally as He will".

Therefore to me the answer to these questions is to be thankful for every gift of the Spirit, to honour those gifts in whomever they are in operation. But the moment anyone calls speaking in tongues (even if only on one occasion) as "*the* baptism of the Spirit", or just "*the* baptism", I think they are going beyond Scripture and laying dangerous snares for believers; for such language unmistakably implies that anything less than that impartation is not *the* baptism; and as we are told that believers are to be baptized with the Holy Ghost and fire, the obvious implication is that those who have not had this gift or sign have not been so baptized, and are coming short of their privileges in Christ. That is divisive language. The moment any of us make an exclusive claim for some special insight or teaching or "revelation", anything which goes beyond the Person of Jesus Himself as the lode-star of our faith, we are schismatics. The gospel is not a doctrine, not an experience, not a specialized anything, but The Person. And if I interpret the gospel aright, we must be large enough to recognize and admire "this same Jesus" in all His redeemed people. I suppose it is only human that we should all feel that the way we see Jesus is the best way and we wish all could share it (as I am doing in this book!). That is right, I believe, for how can any human contain or portray more than a ray of that Universal Light? And we must let what light we each have shine with all its might. But when I say, You must have what I've got, you must see what I see, or else you are not there yet, I am sailing in dangerous waters.

So I still go back to where we started from. The gospel is Jesus in me—by faith. I admire all those who are gifted beyond myself with outstanding gifts of the Spirit. I do not limit the Spirit, but, as I am told to "covet earnestly the best gifts", I lay myself open to take by faith anything He tells me to; but I will not be constrained by man, or chivvied into seeking some special "baptism", because it is implied to me that I am not "baptized in the Spirit" until I do. I have seen many servants of God who have had the Spirit fall on them in special ways. I thankfully recognize every new or special re-equipment He gives. But I am not thereby going back on the walk of faith to say that I have not been baptized by the One Spirit into the one body, when the Scripture says all believers have been so baptized, and that I have to seek some special baptism over and above this one. I prefer to rejoice in the million manifestations of this Universal Person in the beauty and power of His indwelling, yet at the same time giving my own interpretation of Him, *my* gospel, as fervently and emphatically as if it is the only interpretation of the gospel!

Chapter Eleven

Old Man . . . New Man

I think one of the main confusions in Christian living and service is between the "old man" and "new man", of which Paul often speaks. I don't think it is intended confusion. Believers want to be the best for God, and to have correct foundations to their faith, but they also want to be honest; and sometimes they do not feel they can honestly state what the Bible tells them to state, such as, "Ye are dead, and your life is hid with Christ in God"; "if ye be dead with Christ": "likewise reckon yourselves to be dead indeed unto sin, but alive unto God through Jesus Christ our Lord": "your old man is crucified with Him, that the body of sin might be destroyed". The tendency of most of us has been to say, "Well, I reckon it, but it is not really so!" Or, "That is my state in Christ, but not my standing in the world"—a neat rationalization!

Not that anyone wants to rationalize; but how can I say that I have "put off the old man", and "put on the new man"? Aren't I a continual mixture of both, or at least don't I constantly gravitate between the two? James has no use for that, with his condemnation of the double mind, the double tongue, the double motive. But I am sure the problem with most of us is failure to understand clearly what is implied, and therefore experienced by us, in this death and resurrection which we are told we participated in once for all. Where we have got confused is that we are so accustomed to regard *ourselves* as sinful or holy, in the sense that sin or holiness is something ingrained in us; and it is that which causes us to speak of ourselves as having two natures, which we commonly refer to as flesh or Spirit. We regard it that, before we were reborn, sin was a kind of moral infection which permeated our personality; and now that we are reborn by grace, holiness has made entry and partially possesses us, but sin is still there also. We are surely conscious of it, we say, by the rapid uprisings in us of pride, temper etc.; and the constant stirrings of, or at least incitement to, the lustings of the flesh. Holiness is there also; we are new creatures in Christ, and the Spirit bears His fruit in us, but it is a mixture of both.

Our great mistake is the locating of either sin or holiness in *ourselves*. I was tripped up by this for years. I could never come right out with a testimony to an experience of "entire sanctification" or "the purified heart", nor could I preach it convincingly to others, because I always had this question mark. I had entered into a transaction of sanctification by faith; the Spirit had borne witness with my spirit that Galatians 2:20 was a fact in my life through grace—crucifixion with Christ, and He now living in me. But to use such expressions as being holy, or sanctified, or entirely cleansed from sin, or dead to sin, or the old man crucified, did not ring true to my experience, because of my daily consciousness of coming short of

His perfections in some form or other, of sins which need repentance, confession and cleansing.

The trouble, as I say, lay in locating both sin and holiness in the wrong place. It was a great clarifying revelation when I saw that both sin and holiness are basically the attributes of two persons only, and neither of them myself. "Greater is *He* that is in you than *he* that is in the world." Now my attention was directed away from myself to these two persons, the god of this world and the God and Father of our Lord Jesus Christ. I have already stressed this basic truth; but it is so basic, and I think so rarely presented in real clarity, that repetition won't hurt. Put in simplest terms, sin is Satan, and holiness is Jesus. As I have already said, in actual fact there is only one Person in the universe, only one who has ever said "I AM", who calls Himself "the first and the last", who is said to be the "All in all", who is named "the Life", "Love", "Light", "Truth", "Power". We created people are only so created as persons that in a complete sense the living God may manifest Himself through living people, in a way He cannot do so completely in lesser forms of creation. So holiness, love, power, life are never mine, never a part of me, neither now nor in eternity. They always are, and always will be HE in me. My attention, therefore, when I see this, is directed away from myself becoming holy in some sense (and being very conscious that I am not), to Him, made unto me "wisdom, righteousness, sanctification".

But equally, when I have seen with absolute clarity that all I shall ever have of eternal life or heavenly character is HE in me; then it is easier for me to look back on myself in my former unregenerate state, and see just as clearly that the sin was not basically I, any more than the holiness is now. The sin was "he that is *in* the world", "the spirit that now worketh *in* the children of disobedience", the one of whom Paul wrote that he is *in* the unbeliever, blinding their minds. The one who is the false god, who embodies sin which is self-centredness, who is sin, just as the Holy Spirit is holiness. John exposes him to us in the third chapter of his epistle, when he says outright that a person who commits sin is "of the devil", for he was original sin, and Christ came to destroy his works, by replacing him in us; and we have already seen how, when Cain slew his brother, the hater and murderer was within Cain and used Cain as his agent of evil, just as the Holy Indweller, in the next chapter, is shewn using us to express His self-giving love.

Humanity, therefore, always has been and always will be inwardly united to an indwelling lord; it just depends to which. It is not that union with Christ is a kind of novel relationship which has to be got used to after a former life of independent self-living. No, all men are united to an indwelling person; and redemption through Christ means change of Indweller. Satan has been so clever that he has almost totally disguised himself from fallen humanity, so that not one in ten thousand recognizes that he is inwardly motivated by another spirit. We just think it is we ourselves running our own lives! Satan has even managed to get himself smeared and laughed at as a ridiculous creature with horns and tail, so that none recognize the truth of his awful subtlety—that sin is just every form of self-love, expressed through us by the author of it; and as a consequence every breath every unsaved human draws is sin, because it is motivated by self-love, no matter how lofty the deed or character may appear to be: for the only sinlessness possible to humans is Christ in us; He only is that unconditional selfless love which can love God with all the heart and our neighbor as ourself. When the twofold form of union is realized, the one replacing the other, then, as we say, it does not take some strange new effort of faith to recognize this wonderful gift of union with Christ; it is just exchanging faith in the former old union which Paul called being "the old man", to faith in the fact by grace and through identification with Christ in death and resurrection, of the new union, which Paul calls being "the new man".

Now we can begin to get clear between "old man" and "new man". They do not connote any basic change in our human selves. It was the same Jesus who was made sin, died to sin, and rose by the Spirit. It is the same self which reckons itself dead to sin, and yields itself to God as alive from the dead. The difference is not in the self, but in the one who controls and expresses himself through the self. That is why in the same chapter of Romans where we are pronounced dead and risen with Christ, Paul says four times over that we were servants to sin, but are now servants to righteousness. We were always servants in the old life as much as in the new; the only difference was a change of bosses!

That is what clarified my understanding. My attention had been directed away from what *I* was and what *I* had become, to what the Other Person in me was and what He now is. It was no longer a question of whether *I* was sinful or holy; it was a question of whether he who is sin or He who is holiness is united to me. And now I saw how I could with all conviction speak of being dead to sin and alive to God: of the old man being crucified and the body of sin being annulled: of being dead, and my life hid with Christ in God: and how I could use such phrases as "entire sanctification", and "the pure heart". I saw that "the old man" had become "the new man" in Christ, and that therefore they could not co-exist; for the old man was myself joined to the spirit of error, and the new man myself joined to the Spirit of truth, through Christ. I could not be both at once. The death to sin had been a once-for-all fact when I became joined to Christ by faith, and is never repeated, for that was the moment when by receiving Christ, the efficacy of his death which separated him from the sin-spirit became operative in me, and the efficacy of His resurrection by the incoming of the Holy Spirit made the same incoming a reality in me. There is one crucifixion with Christ, and it is never repeated in the believer. Equally there is one resurrection with Him: and in that fact I could say boldly that the old man was out forever (Satan in me), and the new man in (Christ in me): and that is the meaning of "entire sanctification" (separated unto Him as His dwelling place), "the purified heart" (my love-faculty now the means by which He expresses His divine love through me).

Chapter Twelve

What the New Man has to Learn

But that then leads on to the real problem of Christian living—not the old man, but the new man! The wrong use of the new man is the chief sin of the believer, the right use turns life into a magnificent adventure of faith; for the new man then becomes God's battle axe, God's lighthouse, God's intercessor, God's love-channel.

All the training God had to give His chosen vessels in Bible history was not how to eliminate the old man, but how to use the new man. Moses had gone as far as any man in what we would call regeneration, dedication and divine commission when "it came into his heart to visit his brethren"; for the Bible explained what that involved in the most magnificent description of the glory of discipleship ever written (Heb. 11:24-26). Moses' trouble was not a struggle against the pull of the world or the lusts of the flesh, but a misunderstanding and therefore misuse of his renewed self. That was revealed to him by the burning bush. What he saw and learned as a life's lesson at that interview with God was no new thing in Moses; it was only that by "the thousand natural shocks that flesh is heir to", he was at last conditioned to see what had been a fact since he first came into a living relationship with God, whenever that had been—that, not Moses, but God in Moses, was the true new Moses.

Jacob (to refer to him again) is plenty maligned by us Bible teachers; indeed I think that we have far too condescending an attitude in general towards what we deem to be the weak sides of these key figures in Bible history (which is the world's history in its true perspective). How easily we point fingers at the stumblings of the disciples before Pentecost, rather than marvel at the magnificence of their loyalty to their unpredictable Master: and I suggest that a negative attitude towards these men of earlier history, so often making more of their shortcomings than of their dedication, goes hand in hand with the constant belittling of God's present-day church, as if it was ineffective, falling down on its world responsibilities, hopelessly weaker than the devil's counterfeit claimants for world allegiance, such as Communism. Yet the truth is that the church is merely the earthly garment of the Holy Spirit: to belittle it is to belittle Him, as Paul was careful to say when speaking of unbelieving Israel: "not as though the word of God had taken none effect"; and it is far healthier to observe and emphasize the onward march of God's army "terrible with banners", its indestructibility, its persistent penetration, its resilience under the blows aimed for its destruction.

But back to Jacob, the most outstanding example of all, for not one in a thousand has much good to say of his early years. Yet God is "the God of Jacob", and God in Jacob is seen from his earliest years. As Abraham's grandson, who lived his teenage years in those tents of pilgrimage with his grandfather, which symbolized the old man's unwavering pursuit of his heavenly heritage, no doubt the lad absorbed the old man's testimony, caught the glow of his living faith, gazed out with him on the long vistas of God's promises, and determined in his own young heart that Abraham's God was his God also. That was God in Jacob! It was God who constrained him to grab at the birthright so callously spurned by his brother, and we may be sure that that was no isolated incident, but the culmination on Esau's part of a whole attitude of contempt for this other-worldly nonsense. It was God who moved in to rescue Isaac from his one recorded weakness of the flesh, and compel him to give the blessing to Jacob. By a trick? Yes, Jacob had lots to learn about scheming self, and he had to learn it the hard way; but it was Jacob the new man, not Esau the old man, in unwavering pursuit of God. To none other could or would God have revealed Himself, and kept at it until He cornered him at the Brook Jabbok, and Jacob at last learned what Moses learned at the burning bush—that the real new self is God in the self, not self in the self. God is the God of Jacob, not because He has constant mercy on such a failure, that is a libel on the God who lived in Jacob from early youth; but because God had in Jacob the chosen vessel in whom the holy fires could not get quenched.

And so through all the list of these men "great in the sight of the Lord". Their problem was the right understanding of the new man—to use New Testament language. Both the wrong and right use has to be learned. Have we got it clear? We are no longer talking about the "old man", corrupt according to the deceitful lusts. But the "new man" has to be understood, for it is either the seat of all our troubles, or the zestful warrior of faith. The famous "new man" chapter, where its mistaken uses are exposed, is Romans 7. Here it is not the old man trying to do evil, but the new man trying to do good: "when I would do good" (7:21): and we have to learn that trying to do good is the worst sin of the believer. The old man went out in Rom. 6; the real new man (Christ in us) is in action in Rom. 8; the pseudo-new man is active in Rom. 7. It is the three categories of natural, carnal, and spiritual which Paul speaks of in 1 Cor. 2:14 and 3:1. Only natural and spiritual are possible permanencies for a human being; they only are the two natures available to humanity, the natural man having the satanic nature (Eph. 2:2, 3), and the spiritual man the divine nature (2 Pet. 1:4). Carnality is a temporary lapse of the spiritual man: a visit out of Rom. 8 into Rom. 7, whether long or short. Somehow or other the midday sun of revelation has to come out of the clouds and shine in us—that we really are only containers. I am convinced that there are thousands of God's people, redeemed, knowing Christ in them, often having the terminology and something of the experience of the victorious life; but this last bridge has not been crossed, when it dawns on them that Christ is really living His life in them, and that's the end of everything for them. For time and eternity He will express Himself exactly as He pleases by them, and live where and how He pleases in them. Christ has become their true self.

In contrast to this, prayer in pulpit and pew, ordinary conversation, attitudes in crises, betray the normal outlook—that they are living their lives with God's assistance, and what happens to them, happens to them, not to Him. Just here and there eyes have been opened, that's all. Glimpses of Christ in us are seen by all certainly, for that is new birth revelation; but the completeness of the fact, and its implications, no. In the final chapter of this book we quote from the letters of a seeker who became a finder, in order to shew this difference.

It is when this midday sun is shining in us that we see clearly the difference between life in Rom. 8, but visits to Rom. 7; for we differentiate between the human self tempted to act by itself as if separate from Christ, and the Other Self, Christ, acting in us. The moment the human self acts by itself it is in the illusion of separation from Christ, and acts as merely flesh; for flesh is the scriptural word for humanity separated from God through the fall: and flesh not controlled by the Spirit is immediately the dwelling place of sinful lusts (7:18-21). Then here we are, "wretched men", knowing the temporary dominion of Satan in our outer man.

That is the Rom. 7 life. It is the misuse of the new man through the misunderstanding of what he really is. It takes us right back to our fundamental revelation: that the human self never was and never can be independent self. It only imagined it was so in its unregenerate days, not knowing its inner satanic lord and master. But because of this false imagination, we carry over into our redeemed life, into the new man, the instinctive idea that we can be self-active for God now: and we go to it. We *try* to pray, we *try* to love, we *try* to witness, we *try* to keep God's commands, we *try* to study the Bible, and the wheels of our trying run pretty heavily. And as we try, the very opposite to what we aim at gets hold of us ("for in positing one thing, we also indirectly posit the other which we exclude"), and we seem to ourselves more sinful than before we were saved! For we cannot be a vacuum. If it is not Christ in us, then it is Satan; and when we do not abide in Christ according to Rom. 8, and foolishly or ignorantly think that we can live the Christian life under our own steam, then in our soul and body (our flesh when apart from the Spirit) is there the uprising of sin (the self-loving spirit), and our helpless response to it. Satan invades the self that is enticed away from Christ. He does not take over the inner citadel of the human spirit which is in union with God's Spirit; but he sends his soldiers over the walls and diverts attention to himself and claims some temporary footing. Repentance, confession and cleansing in the Blood are the weapons which send him flying again.

Maybe by repeated failures, by the strain and stress of a life we can't cope with, at last God opens our eyes, and we see our mistake. The new man (the human part of it) is as helpless as the old man! Neither was made to function by itself, and never has, and never will. The old man was Satan in us: the new man Christ in us: in both cases the human self is the container, the recipient, the agent. At last we see it; and Romans 7 was as necessary to our spiritual education as the backside of the desert to Moses, and the years with Laban to Jacob. Now we know how to avoid the pitfalls of that subtle chapter. We still pay calls there, but we know where we are when we do, and we know how to get out quickly. Our normal life by grace is now in chapter 8, with the occasional visit to chapter 7; only we must admit that for most of us, and I include myself, the visits are too frequent. We surely never get beyond the daily cleansing of 1 John 1.

Now we are conditioned to understand the right use of the new man. But just at this point we have to be alive to one pitfall. Battered about by our failures through self-effort, we are in danger of pointing an accusing finger even at the helplessness of self. We are ashamed of our weakness. We condemn ourselves for our fears, our shrinkings, our questionings. It is the commonest thing to hear Christians commiserating their feeble and foolish humanity before God. We bemoan the limitations of our flesh, as if flesh was inherently an evil thing. No, indeed. Our weakness is our glory. It is that which necessitates the indwelling of God. That is our claim on Him, as new men in Christ. If He makes weak and ignorant humans, then He *must* be their strength and wisdom, for He only makes empty vessels to fill them.

It is, therefore, a great release when we realize that we are meant to feel our inability. Indeed, it should be our constant reaction in every situation. When it isn't, we are on dangerous ground. It is the wisdom of God which keeps us progressing from problem to problem, from one tight corner to another. The most illuminating autobiographical account of a man who had learned this lesson is Paul's in his second letter to the Corinthians. It scintillates with this truth. It is Paul the human, thoroughly human, radiating Christ. The human sticks right out of chapter after chapter; but, mark you, it is not Paul condemning himself because he was human, and feeling that he needs cleansing from it. It is Paul who has a redeemed humanity through the cross, and is now occupied with Christ coming through His humanity in risen and saving power. It is the Paul of Galatians 2:20, who has finished once for all with his self-centred humanity ("I have been crucified with Christ"): the Paul who is now a cleansed and renewed human ("nevertheless I live"): the Paul whose attention is centred on the Other Self operating through him ("Christ liveth in me"). And he speaks boldly of the flesh, not as an evil thing, but as man's normal human condition: only evil, if given a control it has no right to. "Though we have known Christ after the flesh": "my flesh had no rest . . . without were fightings, within were fears": "there was given to me a thorn in the flesh": "though we walk in the flesh, we do not war after the flesh": and in that flesh, "pressed out of measure", despairing of life, troubled, perplexed, cast down, sorrowful, poor, but "though weak in Him, we shall live with Him by the power of God toward you".

Chapter Thirteen

Spontaneous Living

Why is the realization of union with God essential for daily living? And why must we also know that we redeemed humans are wholly and solely His, spirit, soul and body, and not a half old and half new man? Because we are to live freely, boldly, zestfully, gaily, wholeheartedly. Life is to be to us a great adventure. We are not to be ashamed of calling it a thrill. The commonplace is always to be the fresh to us. The most insignificant, the most obscure is life with a purpose. It is spontaneous living. And it can only be that when two facts are facts to which we need make no further reference, except by way of continuous thanksgiving. The one is that God and we are so one'd that we just live, and yet it is God, and in a sense the relationship is automatic—we just live. And the other is that we are free selves, with no internal enemies lurking within, with no civil war or rival claimants within, free to think, free to serve, free to act, free to believe, free to give ourselves for the world.

For normal living is free-hearted, free-minded concentration on the job in hand. We are not made capable of thinking of two things at once. When we are doing something, we put all we have into it. We cannot, therefore, be thinking directly of Christ at the same time, or consciously communing with Him. We have a sub-conscious realization of His presence, like the flow of an underground stream, and we refer to Him momentarily at any time; but the great percentage of our daily lives is spent, not directly in touch with Him, but immersed in our own affairs. Now if the union, by grace, is an automatic fact, then we do not suddenly come under condemnation that we have thought little directly of Him through the day; but just because He and we are one person, so what we were thinking about and doing was what He was thinking and doing. We never were apart, not for one second; such apartness is a ridiculous impossibility. Wherever we are, He is. He has joined Himself to us—by infinite grace—and that's the end of it.

So we are freed to act as normal men and women, living normal lives; yet it is not really we living, but He: that is our special secret, shared with those who know what we are talking about. We pray, we read the Scriptures, but we are not in bondage. We do not even depend on these, we are joined irrevocably to Him; and even if pressures mean that we can't get the times with Him we would like, again we don't come under condemnation or fall into the false imagination that therefore we are spiritually dry or disarmed; no, not even prayer or the Scriptures are our living water or our armour; these are His changeless self, the real Self in us. As we learn to recognize Him in us at all times, fellowship and communion with Him will spontaneously become the heart-beat of our lives.

But being real humans, we must accept our humanity. We are God's means of entry into the human situation, even as Jesus in the flesh was. Christ is living in the world again in His new body. Therefore, we, as His body, must have normal reactions. We "correspond to our environment": every faculty and appetite has its normal stimuli and response. By that means alone can we be living channels of God's responses, and by them of His revelation and redemption. Therefore we shall always start by normal human reactions, and accepting ourselves means that we shall not constantly condemn ourselves for having them, but recognize them as the stepping stones to God coming through. Do we receive a letter or have something said or done to us which simply isn't fair or just, or which is straight unkind, insulting or malicious? We shall feel hurt or indignant or vengeful. That is not wrong. That is normal. Does someone not keep an appointment, or have we a member of our family always late (never ourselves of course), or do we lose something just when we need it, or does the cooking stove go wrong, or are we delayed in a traffic jam, we shall have just those reactions which all humans have—irritation, impatience, frustration, anxiety—and all are normal. Our physical appetites will be as living as ever—sex, hunger, weariness, and the desires to satisfy them.

It is precisely our human responses to stimuli which gets us into action. Without them we should be humanly dead. But how continuously we Christians condemn ourselves because we feel like this or respond like that, or at least feel we should like to. And yet James went so far as to call enticement by our lusts only temptation; and temptation is not sin, he says, for only "when lust hath conceived, it bringeth forth sin". Temptation is response to stimuli, the very means of arousing us to action. What action? Ah, there is the point.

But before we answer that question, let us get it clear that all normal human responses are listed in the Bible in different places as normal, not sinful. What matters is the use we make of them. Hate, anger, jealousy, fear, boasting, pride (glorying in a thing), envy, ambition (aiming for the highest), covetousness, and of course physical appetites, are all mentioned in different places as rightful attributes, and many of them of God Himself. What I have to understand is that my human responses are the negative to God's positive. I am the have-not to God's have. I am made to be that according to the underlying law of all manifestation—that a positive can only be known in contrast to its negative. Yes and no, soft and hard, male and female, light and dark, all the list of opposites demonstrate that to us. You cannot say yes, without having met and conquered all the possible no's to taking a certain course of action; and the no's are the necessary substructure to the yes. You cannot enjoy a comfortable chair unless its upholstery has a steel or wooden framework. The flesh of a body must have a bony foundation. God who is the Yes of the universe, its love, light, power, wisdom, can only manifest Himself as such through persons who are persons like Himself, yet are the opposite to Him—weak where He is the Strong One, ignorant where He is the Knowing One, self-loving where He is the Other-loving, fearful where He is the Courageous One, and so on. The have-nots, where He is the have. In that sense we are as necessary to Him as He to us, as Paul wrote, "the church, which is His body, the fullness of Him that filleth all in all". Our own reactions, therefore, are bound to be and meant to be negative. We don't like this, we are not willing for that, we fear the other; we are disturbed, impatient, and the rest.

Now the point is, in which direction do we go from there? There are the two possibilities. The old or new husband of Romans 7. We can listen to the law, know what we ought to do, act as if we can do it, and find ourselves doing the opposite, continuing bound to our negative human reaction or stimulated appetite, and now passing over from temptation to sin, by continuing as an attitude or action what had up till then only been a temptation. Alternatively, the temptation, these first negative feelings, become the stimulus to faith. They stir us to the action of "looking off unto Jesus". We affirm Him, as He thinks His thoughts in us, looks through our eyes on the situation as He sees it, handles things Himself. We do not necessarily at once lose the *feelings* of disturbance: that is a soul-condition; but we have moved back by faith to where we truly are and what we truly are—Christ in us. It is not that some change takes place in us, some alteration to our faculties or appetites—of course not; but He Himself is the positive manifested through the negative, and swallowing it up. He *is* the love, the patience, the wisdom, the strength, the holiness expressed through us. It is not that He makes us these things. We remain forever the negative, and thus just as open to these same stimuli from our environment as ever.

This life, therefore, is constant repetition, and not some fixed state in which by some mysterious alchemy a change takes place in us and we shall never have these feelings or temptations again. No, it is a "walk"—a favorite New Testament word; and a walk is forever step by step. That is why those who long for some permanent deliverance from some besetting temptation are following a chimera. There is no such thing in the sense that something happens to us, to our appetites or human make-up, which renders us permanently impervious to temptation along certain lines. The only deliverance is not a thing called deliverance, but a Present Deliverer; and the accent is both on the Person and the present. The gospel is JESUS NOW. "As ye have therefore received Christ Jesus the Lord, so walk ye in Him." Again we say it: it is not a change in us, we remain forever the human negative, and that is not wrong; we are meant to be that; and our human reactions will always be what would naturally please or displease us; that is a right human self (the evil self is when we have accepted that as our permanent way of life, which was the former spirit of error in us). The change is not we, but Christ in us, and our recognition of Him by faith. Because He is fixed in us by grace, we shall not know to eternity how much He sub-consciously is living His life through us, so that hundreds of things in daily life do not touch us, daily answering the prayer that He "leads us not into temptation, but delivers us from the evil"; but there are also many daily occasions when we are conscious of temptation and the negative responses in us, and practice the daily repetition of acts of abiding in Him.

It is equally true that we do sin. We go back under the law, into self-effort, and thus into sin. For this, it is the marvel of God's grace that the letter in the New Testament which takes us to the highest summit of holy living as our normal living, John's first epistle ("as He is, so are we in this world"), starts off with very special provision for every deviation from such a walk. John warns us against rationalizations: don't pretend it is not sin, when it is. Call sin sin, the light of God shining in our hearts will quickly enough expose sin to us. Confess it, and the word confession means "saying with", in other words, saying with God that a sin is a sin, when He points it out! The moment we do that, the blood of Jesus Christ is a greater reality than the sin; it is the positive which has swallowed up that negative. It is a permanent fact, shed in history two thousand years ago, ever held in remembrance before the presence of God by "the Lamb as it had been slain".

Faith, therefore, is entitled at once to replace the reality of the sin with the reality of the cleansing; and it does so. No glory is given to God by remaining in the guilt of sin when the cleansing has been provided. Guilt can become a form of pride and false shame—Fancy me doing a thing like that!—instead of recognizing that we are just the people who will always do that kind of thing, when we forget our abiding place. It is right that we should be humbled and ashamed, but it is more right that we should boldly rejoice in the cleansing blood of Jesus. By this means then we "walk and please God": we live our normal lives freely, Christ in the sub-conscious; in moments of need, stress and temptation, these very conditions are the means of quickening faith into action, faith in Christ our real Self—the life of repetition: when we fail to abide, as we do fail, we move back to the immediate efficacy of the precious blood of Christ, just as quickly as we moved out of Christ into sin; and again we go on our way rejoicing.

Chapter Fourteen

Adversity or Adventure?

Temptation touches us where we need to be touched, for its origin is our own stimulated desire (James 1:14). Temptation, therefore, establishes us in sanctification; it presses us into Christ. It exercises us in conscious abiding; it compels us, by trial and error, to find our helplessness with no hope outside of Christ living in us. We shall continue to be tempted where we are most vulnerable, that is God's right way with us, until at last it dawns on us that appetites do not change, human responses do not change, temptations do not change; there will never be a hope of relief or release, not after forty years any more than after one year, except in the Absolute Other within, who is the Positive that negates the negative, the Light that swallows the darkness. That fact only will stabilize us in the only way of deliverance, the daily walk of faith.

Trials are for another purpose. They come from outside and for outside objectives. They are the normal pressures of life upon us. Right from the time of our new birth, we are told to glory in "tribulations", which in the original means pressures. All of life is surely pressure. The question is why? The answer is redemptive opportunity. Temptations are for our redemption, trials are for the redemption of others. Every negative situation—this need, this frustration, this catastrophe, these difficult people, this church, family, business tie-up, is the very place where light will shine out of (not into) darkness. They are the negative which has as its polar opposite the positive, as south has its north. It is a dialectical relationship, where the two are related to each other, belong to each other and fulfill each other by being the opposites of each other. Need linked to supply, weakness to strength, problems to their solution, and the rest. This is what turns life into adventure; but it is the adventure of faith—not of sight. Disasters, disappointments, shortages don't look like adventure; but it is the same old story. This life is repetition, the repetition of faith. The world which lives on the surface of things must always have novelty, for repetition is sameness and sameness to them is boredom. Children of the kingdom within never have boredom, for the same daily activities are always new; for they are God appearing in new guise for new ventures of faith. The sensational novelist always makes a lot of courtship and marriage; it is something new. A serious writer will examine how forty years of married life work out, for he knows that real life is repetition. Can every day have the freshness of the honeymoon? Yes, every day with Jesus is new, and therefore new with one another.

How can this be? By handling our circumstances in the same way as we handle ourselves or our temptations. We move back from appearances to reality, from the external to the internal. Who puts us in this situation? Man? Devil? Our own foolishness? Our own disobedience? No, that is not taking it far enough. The Bible makes it plain that God as purposively sends the unpleasant as the pleasant. No reader of the Old Testament, or of the comments made on God's foreordination in the New, can call that in question. God's will and its outworking in our lives is not permissive, but determined. That makes a decisive difference to our outlook. When even Satan is only God's agent, and evil men only fulfilling His foreordained plan (Acts 4:27, 28), then we can start off by praising God for adversity, and counting it (not feeling it) "all joy when ye fall into divers trials". That means we have transferred our attention from the situation and our natural dislike of it, to its underlying source, and we only do that by the act of faith. So we are back again to our familiar friend—faith in the absurd—that adversity is prosperity in disguise; and the assaults of Satan, or "the slings and arrows of outrageous fortune", or the contradiction of sinners, when our eyes are opened, are Christ walking to us on the waters.

Paul calls that "always bearing about in the body the dying of the Lord Jesus", and being "always delivered unto death for Jesus' sake". That means that we are accepting unpleasant situations or daily pressures rather than resisting them, even as Jesus accepted Calvary; indeed, that it is He Himself in us continuing His death-process—"the dying of the Lord Jesus"—in our daily lives. This is nothing to do with the death relationship we have with Him in His once-for-all death to sin, which is never to be repeated in Him or us. That death was for our deliverance. These daily deaths are for the deliverance of others through us. That was the death of the old man. These are the daily deaths of the new man. It is not wrong that we dislike difficult situations; it is merely human. But these are deaths to our human reactions. We deliberately accept these things as ways in which God, not Satan or man, is coming to us, and therefore all we can do is to give thanks. "I *take pleasure* in infirmities, in reproaches, in necessities, in persecutions, in distresses for Christ's sake: for when I am weak, then am I strong."

Consider this and come to your own conclusion on Bible evidence. It is important externally, just as it is important internally. We are only free within, if we are unified, Christ and I without inner rival, though there are plenty of attempts at invasion. And we are only free without, if also we are unified: that is to say, if what comes to us comes from one source only, with one purpose. I cannot think that it is sufficient, nor indeed Scriptural, to keep calling unpleasant situations "the permissive will of God". God does more than permit. That is not the kind of God the Bible portrays to us. There we have a God of an eternal purpose. He does not stand by and allow a thing to happen. He ordains it. If He passively permits things, may He not be equally passive about removing them? But if he sends things, then I can at once rise up in spirit and say, Here is a purpose of God. What is it? And I can assuredly start praising, for, "as for God, His way is perfect."

Life is unified. First we see Christ only in ourselves through grace. Then we see Christ only in all men, either shutting men up in their unbelief that He may have mercy on them (Romans 11:32), or being formed in those who have obtained mercy. Finally we see Him only in all things, working them all after the counsel of His own will (Eph. 1:11).

If we have this settled in our minds, and appropriate it by faith in each given situation, then we are ready to ask another question. For what reason does God come to us in adverse circumstances or in contradictory people? The answer is that it is *not* for our personal benefit, for our testing or further sanctification or something. We are so used to relating everything to ourselves in the spiritual life as much as in the material, that we tend to interpret everything in that light—what is God doing or saying to *me* through this? Not at all. God, who is pure outgoing love, has other ends in view. We are now His body, and a person has a body, not for feeding or clothing or coddling, but for using. So Christ in His body. He lives over again in us in all sorts of circumstances to reach others by us. Now that turns adverse situations into adventure. They are not for the dreary purpose of some more self-improvement (an impossibility anyhow!), they are the outflowing of the rivers to others. It is pitiful to hear so often even elderly saints still regarding their trials, physical or material, as some further lessons from which they are to learn, instead of the freshness of the outlook: here is God, even in old age, opening further doors for sharing Him with others.

God is wholly outgoing through all eternity. We have begun that life for eternity, for He lives in us. What a vista! And God specializes in giving Himself for those who are most unpleasant to Him, sinners and enemies; and now He specializes in doing it through us. That puts meaning and content into every possible situation a human can be in. Love is unstoppable. There is always opportunity to love. This is "the life also of Jesus manifest in our body", which Paul says (2 Cor. 4:10-12) always replaces the death. In the death we accept conditions we would naturally reject, and in doing so, we "die" to our reactions. This now makes possible seeing things as He sees them and thinking about them as He thinks; and His thoughts are always redemptive and reconciling. This is the risen and ascended Person living in us. It affects us physically and mentally. Just as the fire of God in the burning bush refuelled the bush, so He in us quickens us, body and spirit. A quality of life is manifest in us, though we may not know it. Faith and love in a person cannot be hidden. The medical profession to-day tell us plenty of the effects of mental attitudes on the physical; then how much more when it is the Spirit of God in us producing the laugh of faith, peace and poise, a relaxed outlook, freedom to bear other people's burdens.

But that is only incidental. Christ's risen life is manifested in our bodies. His ascended life flows out of us to others. So Paul continues, "So death worketh in us, but life in others." We do not make that up. Flowing is effortless. Once we have taken the place of death in daily situations, accepting them as sent of God, there arises in us spontaneously the realization of Him in His outgoing love. He has a purpose for others in this. What? He will doubtless shew us. It will certainly bring faith to birth in us, for the next verse (13) speaks of having "the spirit of faith" (not, therefore, our faith, but the believing Spirit within); and it will be faith that the God who has put us in a place of need already has the supply on the way, for our timeless God has things the opposite way round to us. We think there is the need first, and that we must now seek the supply. God has the positive supply first, and sends the need to be the receptacle for the supply. We talk further of this in another chapter. The negative, the need, the problem, the frustration, is only the means of manifestation of the positive, which was already there. Bible prophecy is one form of the unveiling of those supplies which have been there long before the need, and are revealed "in due time".

So every situation is a situation for faith and love. It may not at all be a matter of a great crisis. It may just be daily living. But as we said, daily living is repetition. Faith is always a necessity, for all life is a series of appearances. Things and people seem to be what our outward eye sees them to be—and that is ordinary, the same, maybe the wearisome, the tiresome, the boring, the irritating, the carnal. But faith sees differently. Faith sees Jesus in them, either seeking the door of entry into their hearts or growing up in them. Faith sees Jesus resolving problems or providing needs that are beyond man. And love means that God has put me just there to love through me, not to pester, not to judge, not to drive, but freely to give myself—patience, meekness, service, sometimes faithfulness; and in the secret of my spirit always "calling the things that be not as though they were".

Chapter Fifteen

Law, not Sin, the Problem

Paul puts a right relationship to law in the forefront of his victorious life teaching. He makes it as important to understand what it is to be dead to the law as to be dead to sin. This is startling, for sin is bad, but law is good. "Sin shall not have dominion over you, for ye are not under law," he says. "The flesh lusteth against the Spirit . . . so that ye cannot do the things that ye would. But if ye be led of the Spirit," you will walk in victory, does he say? No, "ye are not under the law". He puts the law right in there, meaning that it is as important to be out from under the law, as it is from under sin; indeed the two are basically connected. Then, though he admits that "the law is spiritual . . . holy, and just, and good", he vigorously throws it out from the believer's life: "Ye are become dead to the law by the body of Christ": "having abolished in His flesh the enmity, the law of commandments contained in ordinances": "blotting out the handwriting of ordinances that was against us, which was contrary to us, and took it out of the way, nailing it to His cross." Strong language!

Most believers have a partial understanding of Paul's meaning. That is to say, they have it clear that "by the works of the law shall no man living be justified", and that "by the law is the knowledge of sin", and that "Christ hath redeemed us from the curse of the law, being made a curse for us." They understand that law carries a penalty with it, if it is broken, and that we all are law-breakers, but that Christ paid the penalty. Therefore, to that extent, we are finished with law; it cannot condemn or punish us any more. But most believers equally think in some vague way that we are still bound to obedience to law. Is not the New Testament full of commands to be obeyed? Certainly we have moved clean out of the false notion that we are righteous before God by keeping the law, "going about to establish our own righteousness", but we have not moved clean out of maintaining some place for law in the believer's life. But Paul throws it right out, bag and baggage. Not just the works of the law, but law itself: "Christ is the end of the law".

We have, therefore, to delve deeper to get this into right perspective. We have already said that law can be defined as the way things work, and they don't work any other way. At the creation only one law was given to man (the way man works)—the law of receptivity—"eat". But man obeyed that simplest of all laws in reverse, by eating of the tree of self-sufficiency.

Now the situation changed. Instead of eating of the right tree and receiving Him who is love and who would live the love-life through him (which is the fulfillment of all law), he had been taken captive by the huge delusion that he could manage his own life. So now the history of law in our fallen world begins. God in mercy and grace meets man on his new blinded level and says in effect, "You can live your own life? Very well, here is the law. Man is made to love God with all his heart, mind and strength, and his neighbour as himself. Obey it."

In other words, God institutes an elementary and external form of law, suitable to man's condition—the form of "do this and you will live". Twice in the Scriptures it is called man's elementary religion: "we, when we were children, were in bondage to the elements (rudiments) of the world . . . under the law": and "wherefore if ye be dead with Christ from the rudiments (elements) of the world, why . . . are ye subject to ordinances, Touch not; taste not; handle not?"

Law, therefore, was the first form of God's grace, because it imposed an impossibility on man—that the selfish one should be selfless—and gave him the chance of discovering his truly lost condition.

Man's response to law has been twofold. The first response damns, the second opens the door to salvation. The first response is hypocrisy, the second honesty. Hypocrisy means pretending to be what we are not. All men, including ourselves, have done that. We have sought to build our own righteousness and maintain our own respectability by pretending we keep God's law, by keeping a very little of it where convenient: a little religion, a little ethics, and so on. What we really do is to display the one or two commands we do keep, but carefully hide the dozens we break. We cling to an eleventh commandment— Thou shalt not be found out! This attitude finally damns us, because it is not ultimately sin that damns; God has provided for that; it is dishonesty, refusal to admit and confess sin. "This is the condemnation, that light is come into the world, and men loved darkness rather than light . . . and hateth the light, neither cometh to the light."

Man's other response to law is honesty. Recognition that we are all law-breakers. That is the one capacity we have—recognition and admission of fact. That is what Jesus meant in the parable of the Sower, when He said the good seed fell into an "honest and good heart".

Now law, as the elementary religion for humanity, has done its first work. It had compelled those who respond to admit that they are law-breakers, and therefore exposed to the consequences of broken law. Its first work is to produce and pronounce guilt: "what things soever the law saith, it saith to them who are under the law: that . . . all the world may become guilty before God." So far so good. Every sinner saved by grace knows this. But law has not yet finished its work. That is why Paul makes these references to the law in relation to the believer. There was a subtler, profounder purpose in the giving of the law, which can probably only be realized after the law has done its first work. Man's real trouble is not the sins he commits and their consequences, but the root cause of his sinning. That root cause is the spirit of error living in him and having total dominion over him, because the fundamental fact of human nature is its helplessness. Man is created to be possessed. But the spirit of error in him has carefully hidden this fact from him, so that he thinks he is self-sufficient. That was the ground of God's challenge to him through the law: "If you can, do it!"

Conviction of sin and admission of condemnation through the law is really also admission of helplessness; but few see that at the time of conviction, because we are more concerned with consequences than causes. We still labour, therefore, under the delusion that we can do much to serve God aright; and the pulpit is often the worst culprit in making us think so and exhorting us to do so. Even the Bible, misread by those who don't yet understand (and meant to be so misread, till they learn their lesson) appears to be full of exhortations to us to obey the commands of God.

This is why Paul reintroduces law in his statements about effective Christian living, and heads it up in the great law chapter, Romans 7. Most significant is that it follows Romans 6 and precedes Romans 8. It was not put here idly. Paul is following through his masterful train of thought in the whole letter. Romans 6: We, the redeemed, have been freed once for all from our old slavery to our old master in the cross of Christ. Let us now walk in newness of life. How do we so walk? Not under law, but by the Spirit, and Romans 8 outlines that triumphant life.

But wait a moment. Before we can walk confidently in Romans 8, we have a lesson to learn. We have lived under a form of elementary religion, the law; and the law kept telling us to do this or not do that. Why? Because it had a deep and subtle error to expose. We thought we could do things by our own strength, so God sent the law, in grace, to catch us out. We did not do the things we thought we could. We did not keep God's law. But more than that. We *could* not keep it.

Now, said Paul in Romans 7, watch the effect of being "under the law". It says to you: You do this. We say we will and want to (we delight in the law after the inward man). But we find a contrary principle at work in us, compelling us to do the things the flesh wants to do, not the Spirit—and we follow the flesh. We find we are "sold under sin", and that "sin dwells in me". How is this? Because, not having yet fully understood our selves, we have not yet grasped the fact that self-reliant self *is* sin, that is what Satan is, and self-reliant self can only desire to please itself, that is the power of sin in it. But in Christ we are no longer self-reliant selves; instead, we are containers of Him. We are not in the flesh, but in the Spirit. He, who is love, is Himself *the* law, and lives that life of love through us.

Then what has happened? If that is so, why do we experience the bondages and defeats of Romans 7? Because, not having completely learned, or easily forgetting, the basic helplessness of self, and its only function to be the container of the Spirit, we are constantly assaulted by temptation to be something or do something or not do something. Obey those commands, pray more, give more, witness more, be more patient, don't lose your temper, get rid of those evil thoughts, struggle against your lusts, and so on. The real answer to all these is Christ within. He is the Person like this, and I boldly reckon on Him to live like that in me. But because I have been so used through the years to do things for myself, before I know where I am, I have slipped back into the *illusion* of being an independent self, and set about trying to obey that law. The moment I do that, I have slipped back into Romans 7, and am in the flesh, in bondage to indwelling sin; and of course I cannot do the things that I would, and do the things that I would not. It is an illusion that I act as if I was temporarily out of

Christ and under an external law; though the effects of the illusion, the sin I commit is no illusion, but a reality that has to be confessed and cleansed.

So Paul says we believers have nothing to do with Romans 7. It is not a chapter for us, we do not live there. He categorically starts by saying that we are like a wife whose husband has died and so can legally marry another. Thus we have died to the law in the death of Christ, and been married to another, the risen, indwelling Christ. We have exchanged the elementary religion of external law for the adult "religion" of the indwelling Christ who lives the law in us. Having said that in the first six verses of the chapter, he spends the remainder of the chapter describing the condition of those who *forget* they are no longer under external law, or who have not learned law's deepest lesson—to teach us, not only our guilt, but our helplessness; and who as a consequence slip into trying to respond to law's demands, and at once find that they are temporarily enslaved again to the spirit of self-love which has its home in independent self. Thus trying to do good becomes a believer's chief sin, in place of trying to do evil, the sin of the unbeliever.

Law is always with us, as is the flesh, the devil, the world. They are not dead, but we dead to them. Therefore, law is always round the corner to catch us out, and we need catching out until we learn our lesson. Every sort of enticement can be law to an earnest soul. We read a stirring biography. Why aren't we like that? Down we go under false condemnation, because we have allowed an external "You ought" to slip in instead of "Christ is whatever He pleases to be in me". These constant exhortations to be better Christians, even the commands of Scripture, become external law to us, instead of, "Lord, you are all those things in me. Please live them out through me." For the hidden secret of the Bible is that its commands are to the new man, which is Christ in me, not just lonely me. See how John writes, "Hereby we do know that we know Him, if we keep His commandments . . . ." But then he quietly adds, "But whoso keepeth His word, *in* him verily is the love of God perfected . . . He that saith he *abideth in Him* ought himself also so to walk, even as He walked."

In temptation it is the same. Enticement comes, followed by the warning frown of the law, "You must not". If we follow that and try not to, we are back in the bondage of helpless self, and sin in the flesh. The answer is to remember Christ living in us. He is God's "way of escape" when temptations "take" us. The relationship between us and sin, flesh, world, and law, is that between light and darkness. Where is the darkness when light is shining? It is there, yet it isn't there. Withdraw the light, there is the dark. It is kind of swallowed up by the light, as the Scripture says mortality will be swallowed up of life. So it is with flesh and Spirit. We are not in the flesh, but in the Spirit, Romans 8 says. Yet the flesh is there. Where? Swallowed up while we walk in the Spirit. And when it begins to shew its head by temptation, the answer is to reaffirm our stand in the Spirit. Turn the light on, and where is the dark? And so with the world and the devil—and the law.

The use of the word "death" in the Scripture needs understanding also. It is never used except as the reverse side of resurrection. In other words, if there is a death on one plane, there is always a resurrection on another. Death is never dissolution. People can be in bondage because they imagine, for instance, that if they are dead to sin, they should never have any feelings or response again in that direction. But when the Scriptures say that lost humanity is "dead in trespasses and sins", that certainly means dead towards God. But does that mean that God can make no approach to us and we no response? Obviously not. So also when we are dead to the world, and to sin, and have crucified the flesh, it does not mean that we have passed into a realm where such are non-existent and cannot appeal to us. What death and resurrection mean is that we are officially out of one realm and in another. If dead towards God, we are clean outside the kingdom of God, though not outside appeals from it. If dead towards sin, it is likewise. If, as a member of one nation, I change my nationality, I die to my former country and "rise" to my new one; but that does not mean I cannot visit the old country, or be appealed to return. So it is with our new relationship in Christ towards law, sin, flesh, world. Thank God, that means really out of them and really in Christ, though not out of reach of their enticements and solicitations, and sometime paying them visits from which I have to return with confession and for cleansing.

Chapter Sixteen

How Does Soul Differ from Spirit?

When the writer to the Hebrews wrote about there being a "rest to the people of God", he defined it as being a ceasing from our own works. Not from work, of course: that is an impossibility; but from works proceeding from self-effort. In other words sharing God's rest does not mean ceasing *from* work, any more than our ever-active God ceases, but resting *in* our work. Work which has rest at its centre is work from adequacy; work which has strain at its centre (the kind we are most accustomed to) is work from inadequacy. If you go to a store to buy ten dollars worth of goods with only one dollar in your pocket, you buy from strain: if you go with twenty, you buy from rest! If our activities are dependent on our own resources, we work from strain; if upon His, we work from rest. That is also the "second rest" Jesus spoke of in Matt. 11:28-30. He worked from rest, He was so evidently relaxed. Why? Because in lowliness of heart He thoroughly knew His human nothingness, and therefore could also know His indwelling Father's allness; and being meek of heart, He knew how to abide in His Father in times of stress, rather than rushing off to handle situations His own way. So He now says to us: "You are in my service, so learn the secret of rest in work from Me, learn the meaning of meekness and lowliness of heart. If you do that, you will rest, not only in your spirits from the past burden of your sins and their dominion over you, but also in your souls from the emotional stresses of daily living ('ye shall find rest unto your souls'); and then you will be able to prove what now seems a paradox as I say it: 'My yoke is easy and my burden is light', when the normal experience is that a yoke is hard to pull and a burden heavy to carry." God gave me that word personally thirty years ago when I had to take up responsibility in the mission to which I belong. "Watch", He said to me. "Whenever your yoke is hard to pull, or your burden heavy to carry, you are off beam. Get on beam again!" I have found that an excellent barometer!

Now the Hebrews writer takes this further when he distinctly connects the experience of this rest with ability to discern between soul and spirit (Heb. 4:9-12); and my experience is that a great many of God's people are confused and frustrated, and live in a great deal of false condemnation, because they have not learned this distinction.

Modern psychology has invented its own vocabulary for what it considers are the subdivisions of the human personality, such as the subconscious, the id, the super-ego, and so on. But God gave us His own definition and analysis centuries ago, and that will never be bettered.

Man, the Bible says, is tripartite—spirit, soul and body: and in that order of importance (1 Thes. 5:23). In the Hebrews passage, however, it stresses that the difference between soul and spirit is very subtle, and indeed can only be recognized by inner revelation. Only the word of God, it says, applied as the sharp sword of the Spirit to the human consciousness, can pierce "even" to that depth, sever between the two, and give soul and spirit their proper evaluation; only so can we recognize the proper function of each without mistaking the one for the other, and thus enable the human personality to move forward in gear and remain there. And further to underline the depths to which it is piercing, the writer uses the analogy of "the joints and marrow", likening soul and spirit to the joints which give the bony structure of the body its flexibility in action, and the marrow which is the inner life of the bones.

The first essential is a clear recognition of the human spirit as the real self, the ego within us. Soul and body are the clothing or means of expression of the spirit. "God is spirit", said Jesus. God is the primal Self of all selves, the I AM, therefore self is spirit: and God is called in this same letter "the Father of spirits", the human ego made in His image. The human spirit is sometimes described as that part of us which can know God. But it is more than that. It is the essential ego, my human "I am". The Bible tells us that it is our spirits that know ourselves: "What man knoweth the things of a man, save the spirit of man which is in him?" When I say, "I myself", the I is the spirit, the ego which can look out from within, as it were, and knows the myself, the rest of me (soul and body). The dying Saviour on the cross commended His spirit (His true self) into His Father's hands. The saints awaiting the physical resurrection are spoken of as "spirits of just men made perfect", for the true self is spirit.

The self, the human spirit, has three basic faculties—heart, mind and will. The word heart, a term often used in the Bible, is borrowed by analogy from the fact that the heart is the physical centre of the body. It indicates that love is the centre. God being love, that which He fathered in His own image is compounded of love. Love is the fountainhead of the ego. "Keep thy heart with all diligence, for out of it are the issues of life." The human spirit is love, self-love through the false union in the Fall; and when joined to Christ by grace, God's selfless love expressed through the human love-faculty.

Mind, the second faculty, is that by which we know things. Not what we think about things, any more than love is what we feel about things, but the means by which we *know* them. "We have the mind of Christ"; that is why we know Him. "This is life eternal, that they might know Thee, the only true God." Ideas belong to the soul realm, knowledge belongs to the spirit. Many know about Christ, they have ideas about Him—that is the soul: it is something different to know Him—that is spirit. The human spirit is the knower. When the divine Spirit is united by grace to the human spirit, He shares His knowing with us.

The third faculty of the spirit is the will, where the choices are made under the direction of heart (love) and mind (knowledge). At this point the spirit (the ego) moves into action, expressed through soul and body. The will is the arbiter of our destiny. If the choice is for God (such choosing being the compulsions of grace), then the will of the divine Spirit takes over in our spirits, and God with His good, perfect and acceptable will works in us to will and do of His good pleasure. The will of the Spirit issues in the activities of soul and body, the willing motivates the doing; but it is now God's will through our wills.

Here is the human spirit, the human ego, in its entirety—heart, mind, will: love, knowledge, choice.

Now we reach the important point. In what does the soul differ from the spirit? It is the means by which the invisible spirit expresses itself. God, the invisible Spirit, reveals Himself through the Son, "the express image of His person", "the image of the invisible God", "the brightness of His glory". This relationship of Son to Father can help us to understand the relationship of soul to spirit. Thought, word and deed are another trinity, in which the word clothes the thought and gives expression to it. In this same way the soul is the emotions or affections by which love is expressed, the feelings, warm or cold, pleasant or unpleasant. The spirit is mind, the knower. The soul is the reasoning faculty by which the mind can explain its knowledge: "be ready always to give an answer to every man that asketh you a reason of the hope that is in you", there is soul explaining spirit.

Now unless we have a clear differentiation between the properties of these two, we can get into a great deal of trouble, because the soul is the intermediary between ourselves and the world; and it not only channels the spirit to the world, but has the reflex activity of channeling the world back to the spirit. Emotion and reason are wide open, not only to our spirits, but to the world around. Our emotions, therefore, can be very variable. We may like this, or dislike that. This may appeal to us, that repel us—either things or people. We may feel exalted at one moment or abased at another; dry at one time, fresh at another; fervent or apathetic; bold or fearful; compassionate or indifferent. If, therefore, we confuse soul with spirit, we quickly fall into false condemnation. Why are my feelings so variable? Why do I feel cold, dry, far from God? Something is wrong. Why do I dislike this person, or resent this happening? I am wrong with God somewhere.

I am flagellating myself in vain. Soul is variable, spirit invariable. In my spirit joined to His Spirit, I live with an unchanging and unchangeable Christ, and am myself equally unchanging by faith. I am not my soul feelings. I am spirit. But if we had not sensitive souls, we could not be affected by the cross current of human living; we should not be humans. We are to be affected by them, but not governed by them, just as He was "touched with the feeling of our infirmities".

We must be discerning. Many of our soul-emotions are illusory. We are allowing ourselves to be influenced by external appearances. We feel spiritually cold, dead, apathetic, hard, dry. We feel we need inner revival. No we don't. All we need is not to be fooled by our souls! The well of living water has not stopped springing up within us, the living bread in our spirits has not gone stale, the fire of the Spirit (with whom we have been baptized at our regeneration) has not burned low. Look within where you and He really are, spirit with Spirit. There is no change. Don't be fooled by the colour of your clothing—your soul feelings. You and He in you have not changed. Indeed we shall have those kinds of feelings, and God intends that we should have, to stabilize us in the walk of faith. They are useful in driving us back to Him in our spirits. As we learn to walk more steadily in Him, we shall find ourselves less and less bothered by that type of soul-feeling. A whole lot of the hunger people say they have, or need of spiritual refreshment, is at bottom because they are mistaking soul-reactions for spirit-facts. The Reviver is already and always within! There would be much less talk of revival among Christians, if we had learned to walk in "vival"—in the fact of the unchanging life which is the real we, Christ in us.

There are many soul-reactions which we are meant to have, so long as we understand them. Jesus said, "My soul is exceeding sorrowful unto death". He then said in Gethsemane: "If it be possible, let this cup pass from Me: nevertheless not as I will, but as Thou wilt." So Jesus was conscious of a contrary will. Was He wrong? He knew the difference between soul and spirit. With His human soul, He was meant to feel all that was involved in becoming our sin-bearer, and He did. But equally He knew that that was not His real self. His true will was His Father's will within Him, in His spirit. His soul-will was the necessary effect of the satanic pressures on Him for our sakes; but that merely drove Him to the three hours of bloody sweat when His spirit-will, His Father's will in Him, so dominated His soul that He could walk that awful Calvary path as a King. Many a time believers are confused in this respect. They feel they won't be willing for this or that, if demanded of them, or that they are now not willing. Quite so. They are not meant to be. In their souls they are meant to shrink and refuse. That is the natural and right impact of an unpleasant situation on us. But that is not the real we or the real will. The real will is down in our spirits where "it is God that worketh in us to will . . . of His good pleasure." We should not even ask people if *they* are willing. We cannot be. We should say, "You will never be willing. Self cannot give up self. But you can affirm in faith that God in you will will His will, and will take you along with Him."

Recently a lady was talking with me, greatly distressed because she had lost her husband. She loved and served the Lord, but she said she could not accept this blow from His hands, and was rebellious. When the difference between soul and spirit had been explained to her, and that her feelings of distress and unwillingness to accept were just normal, but were not the real self in her; and that she could honestly tell the Lord what she felt, but that, in spite of it, she could affirm against her feelings that the Lord's way is always perfect, all came clear.

In our spirits we are undifferentiated. That is where we are all one person in Christ. In our souls we all vary, and are meant to. That is why the salvation of our souls is a necessity, because it is through the infinite variety of our souls that all the glories of Christ will be seen, each of us manifesting some different facet of His unsearchable riches. But variety means contrast without contradiction. Colours vary, we say clash, but all combine in the amazing spectrum of colour beauty. Music the same. There are disharmonies, but all compose the one great harmony of sound. And so with individuals. One person appeals to us, one doesn't. One we naturally like, one we dislike. Then we feel condemned. Should I not also like that one? Liking is a soul response, loving a spirit response. I love one whom I don't like. He does not appeal to me, I say; but God loves him, and God loves him in and through me. In taking that position,

I have moved back, without condemnation, from soul to spirit.

Just as through our emotions we express love, so through our reasons we express knowledge; and reasons vary, as emotions do. Through the reasoning faculty of the soul we can explain to others what we know, and others explain to us. I cannot know what you know. That is beyond my reach—in your spirit. What you know is peculiarly your own, part of yourself. You cannot share that. But you can give me explanations of your knowledge, which I can in turn discuss with you, and it may be that I too will come to know for myself. My reasoning faculty, therefore, in my soul, is open to all kinds of questionings. Like my emotions, it is open to the two-way influences—of my spirit from within, of the world and men from without. That is why in my soul I may have uncertainty at the same time as my spirit has certainty. One of the best illustrations of that was the father who brought his afflicted son to Jesus. When Jesus said to him, "If thou canst believe, all things are possible to him that believeth", his honest answer was, "Lord, I believe. Help Thou my unbelief"! As he looked at Jesus, and knew the kind of things He had done, down in his spirit he believed, and said so. But as he turned and looked at his son lying foaming on the ground, the reasoning faculty of his soul raised questions, and he was honest enough to acknowledge it. But that did not alter his basic faith. His spirit did battle with his soul and would not submit to its questionings; he fought doubt by affirming faith ("Lord, I believe"), and by asking for help against doubt ("help Thou my unbelief"—although he got the wording a bit mixed up!). The proof that faith swallowed up doubt, and spirit mastered soul, was that he got the deliverance.

It is not wrong for the reasoning faculty of the soul to question and doubt, any more than it is wrong for the emotions to have their varied reactions. In fact the soul reactions are the means of stirring the spirit into action. I have already pointed out that doubt and uncertainty are the seedplot of faith, for we can never ultimately prove anything. That is what puts passion into faith. Coming to certain conclusions in heart and mind, we deliberately believe what we cannot prove. Faith is heart and mind committal. The only certainty possible to faith is the certainty of faith! Doubt and questioning, therefore, is a normal condition of the reason, of the soul, and we must avoid the false condemnation of thinking that there is something wrong with us in that condition. Unbelief is a different matter, for unbelief is not of soul, but of spirit. Unbelief means that, in my inner self, I have decided I will not believe a certain thing. I have allowed my soul-doubts to capture my spirit and enslave my will.

When we understand this balance between the spirit of faith and the uncertainties of reason, and how the reasoning faculty is given us to face squarely all the various possibilities that confront us in life, then we enter with zest into life's dialogues. Is a thing this? Is it that? We are not afraid of the cold winds of scepticism. We are not shaken by questions that seem to disturb our faith. We weigh things up and admit our ignorances and inabilities to produce our proofs. But we don't live in the reasonings of our souls. We move back to where we really are—in our spirits. There, in the place where eternal decisions are made, we affirm what we know and are—by faith. Where reason has helped to clarify and confirm, we are strengthened and thankful, and are more ready to share those reasons with others. Where reason raises questions, we are always willing to consider and learn and adjust; but we never permit it to cross the bridge which is forbidden to it, the bridge of revelation from the Other Side, which has become the bridge of faith, the bridge which is nothing to do with rational concepts, but is a Living Person. In that sense opposing reasons are also our friends, because they only serve to stiffen the sinews of faith. "Whether He be a sinner or no, I know not: but one thing I know, that, whereas I was blind, now I see".

Our souls, therefore, whether in the emotions or reason, are the agents of our spirits, our real selves. They express Him who is the indwelling Spirit in our spirits: whether in the old life, the spirit of error; or in the new, the Spirit of truth. This means that, when it was the spirit of self-love in the old life, what our souls felt or thought in their selfish reactions was largely allowed to govern our spirits: if we didn't like a thing, we didn't like it, and so forth. But in the new life, when our souls channel in world impressions, our likes and dislikes, our doubts and scepticisms, we no longer permit soul to govern spirit; gradually spirit masters soul, so that it becomes more and more fixed as a reflector of God's Spirit.

Chapter Seventeen

God is Seen God

It might be asked, if the basic self of God and man is self-love, yet God's self is eternally selfless love, is there not some alchemy by which man's natural self-love can be transmuted to selfless love? Why do we say that man can never by himself and in himself experience a self-change, and just become a selfless person, a God- and world-lover? On what grounds do we affirm that man by himself must and always will be selfish love, and God alone, and none else, is and forever will be selfless love? And that, therefore, if man is to know selfless love, he can only know it if his self-loving self is yielded to, joined to, indwelt by, and becomes the agent of the self-giving Self of God?

The answer is in the marvelous revelation from the beginning of revelation that God is a Trinity. God never has been The One Alone. If He had been, He would not be love, for love is outgoing. From the beginning He has been the Three-in-One. The Father begets the Son, who "from everlasting . . . was daily His delight". The Son "delights to do His will", saying to Him, "All Mine are Thine, and Thine are Mine". The Spirit proceeds from the Father and Son that by

Him God may dwell in us and we in Him; and as we love one another, His love is perfected in us.

One of the great misconceptions of our evangelical faith is, through ignorance of the significance of the Three-in-One, to anthropomorphize God as a lonely figure, "an old man with a beard", as John Wren Lewis says in his pamphlet, *Return to the Roots*, "seated on a distant throne, instead of being what the Bible says He is, Father, Son and Spirit who is the love-life of the universe." "Of Him, to Him, through Him are all things", "who is above all, through all and in you all".

Wren Lewis, a mathematician and physicist, first attacks the common conception of God as "a Being of immense proportions somewhere 'above' or 'outside' the universe of stars and galaxies, who created it all at some distant date in the past and now supervises it like a foreman", a kind of "Old Man above the sky". Crudely sounding, maybe, to us to whom He is the Father of our Lord Jesus Christ, yet without doubt many earnest believers do have an understanding of Him not far removed from that description: at least we regard Him as a lonely separate Being, dwelling in some remote abode, looking down upon, guiding, judging our world. This sense of remoteness, this carping anxiety as to when and how He is approachable on His distant Throne, when we can be sure of His presence and when not, is the commonest misconception of thousands of believers.

Lewis then points out that the Bible never regarded the universe as "a system of stars spread out in aeons of space, or as a space-time continuum, or anything of the sort", but as "an encounter with persons, a network of persons in relationship. Space, time and matter and so on are abstractions of certain aspects of our communication with each other . . . . The truth is that the universe is, as far as we can ever know, a *personal* reality, a system of encounters between people, and all the stars and galaxies and vast distances spoken of by the astronomer are just as much contained within the universe of persons as are the vast number of molecules and atoms and electrons which make up the air that carries our speech."

That gives us then the "clue to the meaning of God", which John summed up in his one immortal phrase, "God is love". Does that then, he asks, deny the personality of God? No. "To say that God means the creative power of love between people, the power we usually call love, is not to reduce God to any *thing*, but rather to increase our ordinary estimate of love, and that is just what we need to do if we are to see life the right way up".

And then we get to the heart of the revelation: God from eternity has been the Three-in-One, and that God is love. "The most detailed and most practical adumbration of Love's nature", says Lewis, "is the Christian doctrine of the Trinity". I would go further, and say, not adumbration, but the central and sole existence of Love is the Trinity. "Love, this doctrine asserts, is essentially a threefold activity of relationship, involving the exact equipoise of three highly personal activities of Fatherhood, Sonship and Interpretation." God the Father, God the Son, God the Holy Spirit. The Fatherhood of love is giving, the Sonship of love is acceptance, the Spirit of love is the interpretation, the outgoing, "which the theologians call the Eternal Procession: for every love-relationship must be open to the third person—to innumerable third persons. 'In this Trinity', says the so-called Athanasian Creed, 'none is afore and none is after another, none is greater and none less than another'. Giving, acceptance, interpretation are all equal, and if they are not equal there is no love. . . . Similarly giving, acceptance, and interpretation are all severally infinite, spontaneous and eternal—yet they are not three loves, but one Love".

This One, this Three-in-One, is the only self-giving love in the universe. The Uncreated Love. Where one Member of the Trinity is, All are, for the Three-in-One is indivisible; so all things are basically manifestations of the Glorious Trinity. As Browning wrote:

I but open my eyes—and perfection, no more and no less,
In the kind I imagined, full fronts me, and God is seen God
In the star, in the stone, in the flesh, in the soul and the clod.
And thus looking within and around me, I ever renew
(With that stoop of the soul which in bending upraises it too)
The submission of Man's nothing-perfect to God's all-complete,
As by each new obeisance in spirit, I climb to His feet.

Everything serves, for love serves, except where the perverted spirit has control.

We have already seen that in only one respect is God not yet seen as God in His true Self; and that is in created beings, made in His image, whose very creaturehood in all of its wonder of spirit, soul and body, has its permanent being in Him. These are they who have taken advantage of their privileged birthright as made in His likeness and have turned their backs, under the dominion of the first rebel, the author and instigator of this sin of sins, on the only source of selfless love in the universe. They have substituted in themselves the only alternative—self-love; for the moment Lucifer, the author and embodiment of self-love, refused to yield his created isolated self to union with the Uncreated self-giving Self of the Three-in-One, he became the originator and embodiment of a love turned in to itself. Let us therefore get it clear. Love is not a lonely self by itself. From eternity Love has been God the Three-in-One, Father, Son and Spirit, giving, accepting, ministering Love. Created selves could not be or manifest that love by themselves, for love is not one by himself, but the Three-in-One. Therefore created selves can only express self-giving love through their love-faculty, if the Three-in-One, who is love, is united to them and manifests Himself through them.

Chapter Eighteen

Long on Faith, Short on Love

I wonder if we conservative evangelicals do not come short on the love of God. I know I do. For years my main occupation has been with faith. Do I believe God aright? Do I transmit to others "the faith once delivered to the saints", Christ according to the Scriptures? I have no intention of belittling that. Forty years ago I fought the battle through at the university, whether I would stand on the Bible as God's inerrant revelation of Himself to fallen man, despite questions some could raise to which I had no answer. Five years before, as I have already briefly mentioned, just before I joined the army in World War I, a faithful man, a retired Major, asked me point blank if I belonged to Christ. I was embarrassed, because I was supposed to be a Christian, but I had already begun to question the reality of God and Christ, for they meant nothing to me in my daily life. But (and that was the unrecognized work of the Spirit in answer to praying parents), I just managed to be honest enough to admit I did not. That is why I see that honesty is God's one requirement of us.

That admission opened my eyes to my true condition. There could be no kidding myself I was right with God if I could not say I belonged to Christ. How did I know that? Because I had been taught the Scriptures from my childhood. Then if I could not say I was Christ's, there was no heaven for me; and for the first time the truth flashed into me that I was bound for hell, not heaven, and rightly so, for I was unfit for God's holy presence. So, again for the first time in all sincerity, I asked forgiveness for my sins. Into my mind came another simple illumination: why, is not that why Christ died—for your sin? And at once I said to myself, or rather it was the Spirit saying it in me, "Then my sins are forgiven, I need not go to hell. Heaven is my home and God my Father!" Where did that come from? Solely from what I had long been taught from the Bible, and the Spirit now illuminated to me. And not only did the peace of God fill my heart, but my doubts of Him were settled, for I said to myself, "Here is a God that satisfies my highest possible conception of Him—a God who gives Himself as an atoning sacrifice for the very people who hate Him and sin against Him. I can never find a higher than that." And where had I learned that? From the Bible.

I set out on the pilgrimage of faith, not only with a love shed abroad in my heart which compelled me to share Christ with others, but also with a firm foundation in the Bible as God's sole revelation of Himself to man. When, therefore, five years later, my faith in the inerrancy of the Bible was severely assaulted by my lecturers at Cambridge, I came to another Waterloo in my experience. I could not answer some of their objections. But I could and did know that the God of the Bible, the God of saving grace through Christ, was my God for all eternity. He satisfied my heart and had changed my whole outlook on life, and I was not going to be moved from the one medium of revelation He had given us, His written Word. I remember going to my room, and kneeling down, and though I am not given to dramatics, opening my Bible and laying my hand on it: and I made my vow there that I stood by that Book: if it was erroneous, I would be in error along with it: if the God I knew was a big mistake, I would be a little mistake along with Him. If there were portions of the book I couldn't explain, or could apparently be proved wrong, well, to me the rights of the book were so overwhelmingly many, I would be content to leave those questions still unanswered, and boldly mould my life and witness on it. It would be "Thus saith the Lord" to me.

I told my tutor so, a professor of theology in Trinity College. He asked me how I was going to spend my life. I told him of my call to join C.T. Studd in the heart of Africa. "Well", he said, "a naive faith like yours may be alright for teaching primitive people; but I think, if you come back in ten years, you will find that your mind will have changed."

Forty years have now passed. I remain, by the grace of God, exactly where I then was. The Book has opened up infinite riches, from Genesis to Revelation, as it unveils a limitless Christ. Every section of it is its own storehouse of treasure. Difficulties still remain and there are questions unanswered, but they too are as minor as they were forty years ago; and mind, as well as heart, has become deeply satisfied with the rationality of the gospel, as well as with its sufficiency. Face the world squarely on any level, in philosophy, psychology and science; in politics and economics; in problems of society and industry; there is no adequate alternative to the Christian faith worked out in human lives.

But through the years I think it true that faith has outrun love, and in that respect I have fallen far short of the very revelation I claim to adhere to. Nothing could shine out more brightly from the Scriptures than love. Of course all living faith is motivated by love: "Faith that worketh by love". But "*add* to your faith... charity", Peter wrote, with a good list of additions before faith reached its goal in charity! Perhaps that is what it is. Zeal for souls is wonderful. We had it in those university days when the Inter-Varsity Christian Fellowship (I.V.F.) was born in a wave of passionate prayer burden, when groups of us would meet in men's rooms for as much as three hours of prayer at a time; and of bold witness which produced such fruits that the vision was given of a students' witnessing fellowship in every university and college in the world. It was my privilege to start my missionary life with another firebrand for souls, C.T. Studd: I think the small fire was attracted by the big blaze, like to like; and I thank God that "C.T." died with the fire of love to Christ and the world burning as fiercely as in his youth. Paul was like that. In his letter to the Philippians, written from prison, "the furtherance of the gospel" was his occupation. "Christ is preached, and I therein do rejoice and will rejoice": "Many of the brethren in the Lord ... are much more bold to speak the word without fear": "I thank God for your fellowship in the gospel... in the defence and confirmation of the gospel." May my end be like these men! There is nothing that gives me more joy than to have been allowed these years to participate in a "Crusade" like this, the Worldwide Evangelization Crusade which C.T. Studd founded, which still burns with a single flame, to bring Christ to those who have never heard of Him, to see the power of God break into hearts, to see Christ formed in them, to help the church grow up in Him, living and witnessing.

But to faith love must be added. Here I have come short. There are reasons. The gospel has two sides to it—wrath and love. It divides the world into two camps, for as Paul said, it is the savour of death unto death, as well as life unto life. The day of "the revelation of the righteous judgment of God" will bring eternal life to the one, and "indignation and wrath" to the other. It is much easier to have an easygoing shew of love to all, if, as many have, we sidestep the judgments of God, and throw an indiscriminate blanket of acceptance over all. The Bible does not do that, nor those that preach its message faithfully. A love of that nature cannot be the pure love of God in us, for it is false to His Word. We must find another way of love, if it is to be the same as flowed out from the Saviour, Paul, John, and the others. It must have a foundation of faithfulness at any price, yet it must be clothed in a love which is more prominent than the faithfulness. But I think we often have those two in a reverse proportion: faithfulness is more prominent than love.

Though eager to witness and speak of Christ, for instance, I am not immediately at home with the "pagan", as Jesus so obviously was—the friend of publicans and sinners. I think for too long I have loved "souls" instead of simply loving people. I have instinctively had the two-camps approach, and taken it that everybody is outside the Lord's camp unless I have found out for sure that they are in it. I have not sufficiently just loved a person because he is a person, and sought the human touch with him which could lead on to sharing what Christ has meant to me. I shrink from contacts, when I should welcome them and refuse to judge by external appearances.

I think that most of us who know the internal condition of churches and missionary societies and other agencies who hold the evangelical faith, will agree that we have much to learn and practice in our ranks about loving one another. We do not face up at any price to the command the Saviour gave absolute priority to in His last prayer and last words to His disciples. Why not? Again I think that some of it is because we have occupied ourselves in safeguarding the truth, expounding the Bible, regarding each other more as consistent or inconsistent believers, rather than as plain beloved brothers and sisters. I have fellowship with some movements and conferences where orthodoxy would not be named as their premier characteristic (though they are lovers of the Lord Jesus and His Word, but do not give the prominence to the latter that we would), and I have learned many lessons from them in the expressions of brotherly love. While they have welcomed me to minister the Word according to the light given me, they have ministered streams of the love of Christ for me to take back as my portion! Love must be expressed. "Beloved, we ought also to love one another . . . let us love one. another . . . and this commandment have we from Him, that he who loveth God love his brother also."

I have certainly found in my own ministry as a missionary secretary that I have much more commonly regarded my fellow-workers as agents of the gospel working according to certain missionary principles for which this Crusade "stands", rather than as those I love as God loves them. It is really a carry-over of the same outlook towards my brethren as I have had so much towards "outsiders". I am beginning to learn that I don't only love Christ in a person, but the person himself and for himself, because that is the love of God to us, and thus to others through us.

Chapter Nineteen

Can We Take It?

God is love. John said that twice in that passage of his first letter, and it sets the final bounds to human destiny. If a man loves, that is the evidence of his union with God. If a man loves his brother, the invisible God is made visible in that act. That is the last word that can be said—for time and eternity. Love is selflessness. The last rung of the ladder of attainment has been climbed. God is total disinterestedness in what might be to His own advantage. When it speaks of Him vindicating His own righteousness, giving pre-eminence to His own glory, that is not because of what He gets out of it: it is because only in the sharing of His perfections can His creatures attain theirs. It is for their sakes, for the universe of His creation, that He maintains the inviolability of His Throne. Love must sometimes be wrathful, appear self-interested and demanding, appear to maintain its own rights and dignity. Only love can safely do that, just because of its total detachment from self-interest. Can we imagine a Being whose sole occupation for the ages of the ages is to carry the burdens and provide for the needs of others, and when those burdens and needs add up to those of the whole creation? And when the only human race we know of, made to be His peculiar treasure, hates Him, rejects Him, takes all and gives nothing, not even thanks, and often denies His existence? And His answer is to set to work to win them back by giving His life for them!

The summit of revelation is that God has predestined man to be just that. And man knows it. Whether by this devious pathway or that, almost every philosophy and religion that has emanated from the mind of man ends up on the plateau of love. We might say that mankind has finally settled that one point—that brotherly love is the goal. Neither logic nor intuition nor revelation can offer an alternative. That could well be called the light that lighteth every man that cometh into the world.

But pure disinterestedness? Total absorption in the needs of others? Service to others as a debt eternally owed to and eternally claimed by my neighbor? The command, "Be ye also perfect as your Heavenly Father is perfect"? Can that be possible in human experience in this life or the next? No in one way, and yes in another.

The "No" way, in which it cannot be, is the path of delusion trodden by frustrated millions through history, the theme of a thousand religions, the pious aspiration but never realization of moralist, philosopher, idealist—and the butt of the cynic and pessimist.

It is mankind's subtlest self-hypnotism. We can love, we can be friendly, kind, co-operative, they say. Give us time and self-discipline and we can attain to perfect love. Are not we commanded in the Bible to love God and one another? Do not the churches exhort us to imitate Christ—"Be like Jesus all day long"? Do they not spur us on to climb the heights of good resolutions by an admixture of prayer and self-effort? The highest philosophers, returning from their explorations of the good life, tell us we ought, therefore we can.

The roots of self-reliance are so deep in us all, so undiscovered, that only by the hard knocks of experience do we discover our vast error. This mountain of perfect love has no route to its summit! It is inaccessible, unclimbed and unclimbable. Paul makes a revealing comment in Romans 5, as we have previously pointed out, which nicely exposes the eternal and impassable gulf between human and divine love: "For scarcely for a righteous man will one die: yet peradventure for a good man some would even dare to die. But God commendeth His love toward us, in that, while we were yet sinners, Christ died for us ... when we were enemies, we were reconciled to God by the death of His Son". There is a limit beyond which human love cannot go—the limit of self-interest and human approval. We might even die for some one or some cause commendable enough, but it must be commendable to us. But pure disinterested love, unconditional, unrelated to the deservingness of the recipient, is divine. Jesus implied it when He said that man's greatest love was to die for his friends: but (as Paul said) God for His enemies. John said the same when defining love as "not that we loved God, but that He loved us". We cannot love God, no man ever has or ever will love God: only divine love can love Him: for perfect love in the totality of its self-giving is so fearful, so devastating to anything less than perfect love, so offensive to self-interested love, that man can never love God, though he may often imagine and say he does.

That is the "No" way. Perfect love cannot be obtained that way, despite the pathetic fact that the world through its centuries of its history has tried to proclaim that it could and does: and that is true, not only of human philosophy from Plato onwards, and of all non-Christian religions; it is also tragically true of the perversions of the gospel by "the works of the law" which Paul and John and the other apostles had to combat even in New Testament days. It is seen in the mixture of self-effort and grace through the writings of many of the Fathers: it found the fullest of perverted expression in the good-works Pelagian teaching of Rome, until the fallacy was so gloriously exposed and combated by Luther: yet only to have returned again in multitudinous subtle forms from the Protestant pulpits. A masterpiece of clarification on the subject is in the book *Agape and Eros* by Anders Nygren.

The "Yes" way, however, by which such perfect love can be attained is made plain in the Scriptures, and has been preserved in purity of teaching and experience by "the little flock" through the history of the church. Of course it has. God has never left Himself without a witness. I have already given the grounds of it in the revelation of the Trinity: the Three-in-One. Here is divine, uncreated, spontaneous, unconditional, undeserved love. But here is the only such love in the universe for time and eternity. He only is love. That is the point at issue. Not half of one percent of admixture is possible. Human love—the love of the independent self apart from God—is the crippled growth of a monstrous birth. It is the use of the love-faculty for self-interested ends, instead of it being the means of the radiation of the selfless love of God; for, once again, its birth was when the first created being, Lucifer, refused to fulfill the only purpose of his creation and be the container and manifester of Him who is selfless love. Cutting himself off from union with the Three-in-One, it was inevitable that his created love faculty turned in on itself to be occupied by self-love. This immediately became its fixed nature. It could not be otherwise. Every outlook and instinct from henceforth was permeated with self-interest. Selfless love was an eternal impossibility to him: and when Adam received the satanic spirit into his spirit by partaking of the tree of disobedience, it became equally and eternally impossible for any human being born of Adam to express anything but self-love. No matter what heights of idealism or religion were aimed at, the basis would always be self-love, for creature love can never rise above its source any more than water can, and can never change itself into uncreated love. *Eros* is of an eternally different quality from *agape*, and never merely a variation in quantity.

But now we see the glorious end-purposes of God. They are that we humans are an eternal expression of the divine, by the fact that He who is love has joined Himself eternally to us and us to Him, in Christ. *He* is love within and through us.

But that means that we redeemed people are paddling in the muddy shallows when we are so constantly concerned with what benefits we receive from Him. It indicates the accursed admixture of this *eros* and *agape*. It means that we in our human selves are seeking something for ourselves, blessing, guidance, power, holiness, cleansing. The very seeking is a form of self-effort, of *eros*. Whereas the real truth is that He has found us, made us His dwelling place, and lives His own life in us.

What then is a totally committed Christian? He has ceased to be his own—neither people, possessions, nor life is his. All he has is Jesus. And what kind of person is Jesus? Unconditional love. Life's occupation, life's absorption, is expressing the love of Jesus in our world. Nothing one iota less. To me to live is Christ—all things counted refuse that I may win Christ (not by effort but by faith that He is what He is in me): and that means the life He will live out in me will be a participation in His power, His vicarious sufferings, and His death for sinners and enemies.

That is this life—Christ formed in us—no question about uncertainty of consecration or doubts about His permanent indwelling: no pursuit of personal revival, refreshment, renewal: but the clear recognition of this unchanging Other Person of love who has begun to live His eternal life of self-giving love through us. This has become our adventure for eternity, the upspringing well and the outpouring rivers.

See the way John takes us to the summit of living in his first letter. He tells that he is going to lay bare to us the meaning of eternal life, which is Jesus Christ—and its implications for us who are joined to Him. He leaves no room for second-rate standards. He says we are to walk in the light as He is in the light, to walk as He walked, be righteous as He is righteous, purify ourselves as He is pure; for as He is, so are we in this world! This is no gospel of standing, but not state! Of imputed but not actual righteousness! Of reckoning but not reality!

Then how can it be? Nothing could be simpler. Keeping His commandments is a consequence of being *in* Him, and a proof of His love perfected *in* us: ceasing from sin is due to abiding in Him: loving the brethren is the same as saying that God dwells in us. That whole passage of 3:7-21 cannot be matched in the Bible in its presentation of the nature of God and the new man. It even surpasses 1 Cor. 13 in that a cause is more fundamental than its effects. A redeemed man must love his brethren. Why? Because being born of God he is born of love. God within is his new nature. God's love is no idle phantasy, for it is plain for all to see in the gift of His only begotten Son to give us life at the price of His own, and Himself pay the penalty of the wrongs done against Himself. This kind of love, reaching out to save the whole world, is the way He now loves others through us, and its manifestation in our love for each other is the only way God is seen by men. What could say more plainly that other-love, self-giving love is not of mere man, but God in a man? And be it noted that this passage which completes and consummates the declaration of the whole letter—that God who is light reveals to us in plainest outline God who is love—is saying not one word to us about His loving us for our comfort and benefit. It is saying that if the marvelous union-relationship is a fact, if we dwell in Him and He in us, then He cannot but live His own quality of life in us—of love, truth and holiness. Let us see then that we live that life, and there is no difficulty at all: for we live by faith, and faith is the recognition of the fact of a Christ who conquered the world and the devil, and that the Conqueror is within us.

Chapter Twenty

A Man Who Lives the Sermon on the Mount

A friend of mine has been showing me God in a man recently, in the kind of experiences in which we admire Jesus most, but follow Him least: in the cross rather than the resurrection, in failure rather than success: "as poor yet making many rich; as having nothing and yet possessing all things". Young, successful, prosperous, and proud of being a good Christian and churchman: a commander in the U.S. Navy in World War II, chief of the Naval Reserve in his city, chosen as the young man of the year, head of the Junior Chamber of Commerce, with a considerable income from the insurance business (in which he was one of four partners) from which he, with a pleasant feeling of how well he was serving God, regularly put his weekly tenth of fifty dollars in the church plate; and with many other prosperous investments in real estate and other interests. But in his heart was a cry for reality—at any price: and His heavenly Lover, who put the cry there, had the satisfying answer—by fire. An eternal marriage was to be consummated, but only at the price of all true marriages: "Forsaking all others, I take thee".

Eight years ago his wife developed schizophrenia.

As it worsened, it took the form of going to lawyers, fellow-deacons and friends of my friend, and suing him for divorce on the ground of adultery. Three times she did this, each time unknown to him, the first information he had of it being headlines in the city newspaper: "Civic leader sued for divorce". The lawyers who took her case, though friends of Jim, always had to drop it because of her mental condition, and the fact that she was hospitalized for it demonstrated its futility.

But it was at this point that the new reality of God in Jim began to be seen. He went to the first lawyer, friend and fellow-deacon, in amazement that he could do such a thing as accept the case behind Jim's back. At first the lawyer refused to speak with him on the legal ground that there must be no communication with the defendant. Then when the case fell through without ever coming to court because of the mental condition of the wife, and Jim again spoke to him, he said he saw now that he had no grounds for taking the case—but his fee was $500! Jim took his check book and paid. Why? Here was the secret. God in Jim had only one concern. The need of the lawyer. The fact that he had so wronged his friend and then dared to ask Jim to pay the fee for his wrong doing, was not the point with God in Jim. That is the kind of way the whole human race has been busy treating God through the centuries. The point was that God loves that lawyer and somehow will bring him out of the inner turmoils of his selfishness and worldly acquisitiveness to life's only reality—God Himself. By some means God will crack him open, and Jim knew that he would not be a channel of that love of God by personal recrimination, claiming of his own rights, refusal to pay the unjust fee. That would turn the attention of the lawyer to Jim and his rights, and not to Jim's God. But by fulfilling Christ's word, "If any man take away thy coat, let him have thy cloke also", and by his own witness that he loved him, God was shewing that man a quality of life and selflessness a thousand miles removed from nominal Christianity, and which all men know in their hearts to be the truth. It was the same method by which Stephen's attitudes and actions brought inescapable conviction to religious Paul. Flesh is not convicted by retaliating flesh, but by its opposite—Spirit.

But this was only the beginning with Jim. Far "worse" was to follow. An ultimatum was suddenly presented to him by his two partners in his insurance firm. Those constant accusations of unfaithful living, publicized by the papers, they said, were damaging their reputation. Also Jim was giving too much time to some of his Christian interests, which were too far beyond the pale for a respectable church-goer. Jim must either get rid of this troublesome wife by divorce and curtail his evangelistic activities, or resign with one year's salary, renouncing his rights to a partnership of which his share was worth around a quarter of a million dollars. Jim had already seen God's word about divorce. He refused their requests and signed the document they presented to him. The fourth partner, not active in the business, when he heard of this, indignantly pointed out to Jim that according to their constitution it took the votes of three of them to oust a fourth, and they would not have his vote; therefore it was illegal and he should sue them. But Jim refused. If God was shutting him up to Himself this way, he said, by causing men to act unrighteously towards him, all he wanted was the reality of God; let Him do what He would: and anyhow he had the word of Jesus against resisting evil, and what mattered to him was that he loved these men and saw their need, and could show them the love of God best by refusing to fight them for this world's goods, convinced that somehow God would reach them as He was reaching him.

What started with a trickle of misfortune soon became a flood; for when it was known that he had been put out of his lucrative job and partnership and had thus lost his security, banks and others who had lent him money for various projects, closed on him. He was ultimately brought to court over a small sum owing, and unknown to him, by a lawyer's trick, and it was turned into bankruptcy. Even there the judge gave him a chance to plead his case and a lawyer was willing to help him, but he simply told the judge that all he had was God's and if God wanted to take it from him through these men, he loved them and it was "O.K." with him. His $40,000 home was taken, car, furniture, investments—all. Money was allotted to the wife for herself and the children, whom she took to another city (though they keep in touch with their father by letter), and the lawyers' huge fees absorbed the rest.

Much more could be told, such as an opportunity he previously had to build a big motel in co-operation with a Christian brother, who agreed that it should be built and run to the glory of God—until Jim found that, for a profit of several millions, this man was linking his chain of motels with those who would sell liquor and permit loose living. When the man went ahead with signing the agreement, though knowing, as Jim pleaded with him, that he was turning his back on God, once again Jim resigned his rights and returned him the document which gave him the authorization to build the motel in that area.

Jim is at present living in a Y.M.C.A., waiting for God to show the next step. Doing nothing? His days are filled with people in deep need who come to him for spiritual counsel, and time and again go away with Christ. What he gets (from the Lord) in his poverty, he shares with those needier—to the clothes off his back. Jim has paid visits to our Mission Headquarters. To be comforted and helped? No, to be a stream of blessing to us, as we see the peace of God and joy of the Lord radiating from him, and learn at his feet. He can do nothing but constantly thank God for using this way of breaking up his self-sufficient self, his pride in his own religious life and standing: for "the cruse of oil" and "barrel of meal" which have never failed: for the provision for and love of his children though separated from him: for the presence of God which fills his heart to overflowing: for the marvelous opportunities of living and helping others which are constantly his, so that, with God's love flowing from him, whether the contacts are with truck drivers or top business executives, their hearts are opened as he tells them what the Lord is to him and they are soon sharing their burdens with him.

One early morning, before all these disasters had overtaken him, he was led to pick up in his car a burly-looking negro, shivering by the roadside. He might have guessed from the looks of him that his history was not savory. But God told him to do it. He took him and kept him for three months in what was then his lovely southern home. Folks warned him that the man might do anything to his children (and he turned out to be an ex-convict): but Willie, the negro, loved them and willingly worked in the home. One day he took Jim's car to the city to buy provisions, and, Jim says, God told him he would not return. Some hours later there was a call from the sheriff, a friend of Jim's: Willie had been picked up in Jim's car. Would Jim put a charge against him? No, Jim said, God had not told him to have any man put in prison. The sheriff banged down the phone in annoyance. Weeks after, Jim met Willie in the streets of the city—in Jim's car. God said to Jim, "Take him home and give him the title to the car". Jim did so and hardened Willie, who had had former bitter disillusionments with religious people, with tears running down his face said, "Mr. Jim, this is the first time I have seen God in a man". Later on Jim again met him—in another car. He talked long with him and Willie seemed to come near a decision, but could not face it, though warned by Jim that if he did not come now, God who loved him and was determined to save him would have to take him a harder way. And so it turned out. Willie was traveling in a stolen car, and is now in a federal penitentiary, for he turned out to be an escaped prisoner. But what letters he writes Jim! He got the warden's permission to have Jim as his correspondent. At first, in his crude handwriting and misspellings, he kept asking for prayer, saying that he knew he was on the wrong trail; and finally the break came and the light shone. He began to rejoice in the cleansing blood of Jesus, confessing his sins, his illegitimate children, and his desire to return to his true wife. Now, with letters continuing like that for many months and the very change in the handwriting showing the change in the man, he is about to come out of prison, and says he wants to come and work for Jim "with or without pay". Jim has the true sense of values—that Willie was of infinitely more eternal worth than many cars.

A strange story? Uncomfortable to read? Absurd and fantastic? I am sure many readers will say so; but true anyhow, and I can put anyone in personal touch with this humbled man of God. It sounds mighty like the Sermon on the mount. If the one is crazy, so is the other! We are not saying that God does exactly the same things through every life. God is original, and we are not called to be imitators. But the principle is the same: that God, as love, is the total self-giver, interested only in blessing those He loves, though they hate and mistrust Him: and love finds means of expression in action, as it did in Jesus, so that our world may see that God's love *is* self-giving, not self-seeking. If God lives in us, we may therefore be sure that He will express Himself through us in forms of self-giving which the world will call crazy and the flesh will always hate. Of course he is misunderstood. His own fellow-church members, his pastor (who used to pat him on the back as his most reliable donor), think him crazy as he sits Sunday after Sunday in the same congregation among his former wealthy friends. But here is God in a man, the very God who Himself endured the contradiction of sinners; who when He was reviled, reviled not again; who was led as a sheep to the slaughter, and as a lamb before his shearers opened not His mouth; who prayed in His dying agony, "Father, forgive them for they know not what they do."

Chapter Twenty-one

Prayer and the Fourth Dimension

I believe a fresh approach to prayer is needed among many of us. The trouble is that we Bible believers, just because we tenaciously hold fast to "the form of sound words", as Paul instructed Timothy to do, are in danger of interpreting in terms of this-world's concepts what are really the data of another world. The Bible can only use human language to express superhuman facts, so that it can be only shadow language; and if we are too literal in our interpretation, we can easily miss what it is meant to convey, just as the Jews failed to recognize the Christ when He came. The inner truth is there like a kernel in its shell, like the living God veiled in the incarnation.

The greatest failure in this respect is in passing over from the unreal sense of separation which this world conveys to us in all our relationships, to the actual reality of union, the Christ-in-you reality which Paul named as the mystery of the ages. In our average evangelical preaching we have rightly stressed separation from God through sin (although we have missed the fact of the union with Satan): we have proceeded to reconciliation through Christ: but we have rarely gone right through to unification of Spirit with spirit. And the reason is obvious. It takes us out of our depths in this three dimensional world of length, breadth and height, of line, plane and cube, where every person or object in its apparent existence is distinct from another. To talk of Christ in us, and we in Christ: to speak of multitudes of persons being one in Him: to be told of a day when everything will be gathered together in one: when God will be all in all: when time will be no more: when past, present and future will be all the same in Him who is already "the same yesterday, to-day and forever": to be given multitudes of instances and statements in Old and New Testaments to prove that future events are already in existence in God's sight, for He "declares the end from the beginning"; such facts and statements are uncomfortable to us in our down-to-earth world of space and time; and even though we accept them from the Scriptures, we really regard them as vague, rather unreal, spiritualities, rather than the actual facts, while what we call real is in truth the unreal!

Our complacency is being shaken, however. If we haven't really accepted the Bible as speaking scientific truth on these subjects, we have suddenly had to wake up to an unexpected ally to the Scriptures—modern science! We find the real, as we see it, is the unreal! Solid matter, for instance, is actually billions of whirling units of energy—whatever that may mean. The empty air is crowded with myriads of sound waves. We laugh at our forefathers for thinking that the sun went round the earth; but we are just as big fools in our misconceptions. And what does all this tell us? They are broad enough hints to us to take heed to these strange Bible statements. There plainly is another world beyond our world of senses.

Some speak of it as the fourth dimension. The Bible calls it the kingdom of heaven. A book, not written specifically from a Christian standpoint though it comes to some near-Christian conclusions, but which is profoundly illuminating on this whole subject, is P. D. Ouspensky's *Tertium Organum.* The title sounds as if it is for the expert, but the ordinary reader can follow right along with it. The point, most carefully argued, is to shew that all we know of the world we live in is merely the interpretation our senses convey to us. Not one person claims to know our own world, still less the universe, as it really is. Speaking of the dimensions, he shews how the first dimension, which is length, is represented by a straight line made up of an infinite number of points: the second dimension, length and breadth, forming a flat surface, a plane, is represented by a square, which is made up of an infinite number of lines side by side: the third dimension, in which we live, has length, breadth and height, and is represented by a cube, which is made up of an infinite number of square surfaces as it were piled on top of one another. Thus each new dimension is composed of an infinite combination of the objects of the previous dimension.

Now what about a fourth dimension? The Bible speaks of it as "the powers of the world to come" (Heb. 6:5). Where do we get a hint of it? In time, says Ouspensky. And the Bible says: "The angel . . . lifted up his hand to heaven, and sware by Him that liveth for ever and ever . . . that there should be time no longer" (Rev. 10:5, 6). What do we mean by time? It is our way of describing what appear to us to be passing events. Time is our point of view on events. Such and such takes place between 6 a.m. and 6 p.m., we say. But there are already some very strange discoveries, as science penetrates farther and farther even into our three dimensional concept of things (which is the limit to which human logic or finite mathematics can take us). For instance, we would think that every object preserves the same dimensions of length or mass whether in motion or rest, and that a clock keeps the same time. But science can now prove that "a clock slows down as its velocity increases, and a measuring rod shrinks in the direction of its motion", but as it is also proved that light, travelling at 186,000 miles a second, is the highest attainable velocity in the universe, it means that a clock travelling at that velocity would stop completely, or a measuring rod would shrink to nothing! It sounds absurd to us amateurs, doesn't it? But Einstein pointed out "that common sense is actually nothing more than a deposit of prejudices laid down in the mind prior to the age of eighteen. Every new idea one encounters in later years must combat this accretion of 'self-evident' concepts".

Why do I quote this? Merely to impress on us that even by finite scientific investigations a realm of "reality" is being opened up which is totally unreal to our human third dimensional senses. We amateurs may well say that Einstein's concepts, his "General and Special Theory of Relativity", leave us bewildered; but this much we do know, that he and others have opened a realm of the inconceivable which is simple fact: we know it because we know atomic power and radio. Riemann, the mathematician, is quoted by Ouspensky as saying, "The material atom is the entrance of the fourth dimension into three-dimensional space". Our three dimensional minds cannot by reason, logic or science, in other words by our normal mental faculties, transcend our three dimensional outlook; but we can see hints of some other inconceivable form of reality, and believers in the Word of God can see it stated there, not for intellectual enlightenment, but for present-day experience, "tasting of the powers of the world to come". That is why this apparent digression into science will be seen to have direct connection with prayer.

What are we learning then? That there is another world besides our present one, which functions on principles wholly different from ours: that glimpses of this fact are observable even to the natural man through philosophy and science, only proving that God does not leave Himself without witness: that an understanding, an experience, and an actual life lived in the power of this other world are available to the believer.

Let us look at it this way. Ouspensky illustrates it by comparing the understanding of an animal with a human. An animal has sensation and perception, but not conception. A human has all three. That is to say, an animal can feel and perceive things, but he cannot conceive why or how a thing is so. He cannot generalize, and thus relate one thing with another intelligently. He has not the powers of deduction and induction by which he can organize, improve, change, theorize on the life he lives. The consequence is that he can only accept things as he sees and feels them. When we travel in a train, because we can think and have concepts, we do not accept the evidence of our senses that the countryside is racing past us. We know that it is we who are moving. An animal does not know that. He must accept things as he sees them. That is why a horse shies at what appears to be coming at him. An animal lives a two-dimensional life. He only recognizes flat surfaces. He does not know thickness, because thickness is a concept. No one has ever seen thickness. All we can see is the six outside surfaces of a cube. We can't see the inside; but because we have powers of thought, we conceive its solidity; we combine the sensations of weight, density, resistance, and call it solid. Now the point of this is to see how, on each level, in each dimension, we can be fooled by our senses. Because an animal has percepts, but not concepts, he is mistaken about many things. Because we have percepts and concepts, we can draw conclusions an animal cannot, and can avoid some of his mistakes; we can have a third dimensional outlook which makes our world of solids into some intelligible whole, and can improve and adapt it to our uses. But we can equally be fooled! The solidity of objects when they are really a whirling mass of electrical charges, the emptiness of the air when it is full of sounds, the disruption of our age-long confidence in the fixity of time and measurements, are evidences of this.

What does the Bible tell us? That there *is* another world-to-come, another dimension if we like to use a human term, and that some characteristics of it are revealed in dim outline, but clear enough for faith to grasp and to live by, or at least greatly to influence our outlook and conduct in this life; but that they are bound to run contrary to our normal three-dimensional outlook, and will usually meet with ridicule, or at least with a push-off as too starry-eyed for this competitive world.

The first characteristic is that persons in this new kingdom are not separate as we regard persons here but are really One Person. But because He is the All, all opposites are resolved in Him; therefore a part may contain the whole, as much as the whole contain the part. Thus the redeemed are all one Christ, yet a complete Christ is living in each!

God is the Three-in-One, One God, yet each Person of the Trinity is separately and distinctly complete God. God the Father, God the Son, God the Holy Ghost; and of Christ it is said, "The Word was with God, *and* the Word was God" and "in Him dwelleth all the fullness of the Godhead bodily". The Whole is one God, and yet the Parts are each the Whole! To human logic an absurdity: to faith a reality. And we redeemed humans are already introduced to this relationship, to this fact. We are actually part of the Ascended Christ: "as the body is one and hath many members . . . so also is Christ". He is the one, complete Christ, the All in all of the body (Eph. 1:23); yet we remain forever separate persons in that One, and in each of us lives the Complete Christ! That is fourth dimensional logic!

A realization of this by believers gives a new sense of solidarity to our unity in Christ. We actually are one person, and Paul prays that our knowledge shall be increased to the point that we realize we are "one perfect man" (Eph. 4:13). This is already the fact, though not realized by our outward senses. It makes an absurdity of separation between believers to the point where we say we cannot have confidence in so and so. We may have plenty of differences between us, owing to our finite minds and easily-disturbed hearts; but basic division, no. If we have, we have divided with ourselves, we have no confidence in ourselves, or worse still with Christ, who is the real Self of every believer. As Paul asked, not, Is the church divided? but, Is Christ divided? (1 Cor. 1:13). I live in a large community of about eighty, at the headquarters of our Missionary Society; and the more closely we live together, the more room there is for personality differences: and I have found this the only basis of brotherly love—that <u>we are one person, though many, and that we love each other eternally as part of the one Christ, who also lives in each of us as our real selves.</u>

Then there is the time question, already mentioned, and an understanding of this from a kingdom of heaven, a fourth dimensional outlook, brings us right up to the prayer question with which we started this chapter. Put together scattered statements in the Bible. "The Lord God Almighty, who was, and is, and is to come". "I am Alpha and Omega, the beginning and the ending": "Jesus Christ the same yesterday, and to-day, and forever": "I am the first and the last": "I am God, and there is none like Me, declaring the end from the beginning". Consider all the prophetic statements: "Christ . . . who verily was foreordained before the foundation of the world, but was manifest in these last times for you": "Chosen in Him before the foundation of the world": "Having made known to us the mystery of His will . . . that in the dispensation of the fullness of times He might gather together in one all things in Christ": "For whom He did foreknow, He also did predestinate to be conformed to the image of His Son": "And sware by Him that liveth for ever and ever . . . that there should be time no longer".

Then time is only a human convenience for spacing out events as they occur. Eliminate time, and what have we? A continued unbroken series of events from eternity to eternity, with past, present and future all one, with neither the past non-existent nor the future still to come; all the activities of the One God who is the beginning and the end. Incomprehensible? Certainly to our three-dimensional minds, who can only live in an actual restricted present, like a horse in blinkers, to whom the past is finished and gone, and the future not yet in existence, and true realities are only what we are passing through now. But that just does not fit with what God has said of Himself in the quotations above, or what is said of Christ. It is plain that God sees the future as already there, and speaks and acts accordingly. Election and foreordination were deep in the consciousness of the Saviour, Peter, Paul and John, with continual references to them in their speaking and writing. Once again, with logic, the question is at once raised: if there is election, where is there room for freewill? And we are again pressed on beyond human logic which can only think in terms of opposites (if there is black, there is white; if there is yes, there is no), to the fundamental unity in God where "separateness and inclusiveness are not opposed, but exist together and simultaneously without contradicting one another": and the answer is that election and freewill are only two sides of the same fact, election in God works out in the freewill of man.

So now, while the world must think and move in

time, living in a succession of events, with the past a mere memory and the future unpredictable, the believer has the veil at least slightly lifted on to reality. He has been introduced to the timeless world, where past, present and future are eternally one and in continuous existence. He knows himself, through grace, to be organically united to the living Christ as branch to vine, and thus also as branch to branch; yet the Vine is also in the branch.

Two further considerations may help us to understand. The first is only an analogy. We quoted Riemann as saying that "the material atom is the entrance of the fourth dimension into three dimensional space". In saying that, Riemann was not suggesting that his fourth dimension was equivalent to the kingdom of heaven we are speaking of. He was speaking purely of the atom being a new dimension on the material plane, because its existence and functions are unobservable and "out of this world" to our normal human third-dimensional senses. In that respect, simply as an illustration or analogy, it can help us to understand the new form of consciousness necessary to move from the earthly dimension to another, the heavenly; from the material to the spiritual, which, as the Bible puts it, necessitates a new birth, a new creation. With our ordinary senses we simply can't conceive or imagine that every object, solid or liquid, in our world is a mass of electrical charges moving at incredible speeds. It just doesn't make sense to our senses. Equally we have to take it on good authority that, while we appear to be comfortably and securely at rest on our planet, we are really whirling round our own axis, and our earth racing round the sun, and the whole of our solar system rushing through space at thousands of miles an hour. Once again it doesn't make sense to our senses. The same with all the sound waves speeding through our apparently still and silent air. We can see then that in a certain condition of consciousness we can be completely at rest, and can utilize for our convenience innumerable solid substances, when in reality to another level of consciousness there is not one thing either solid or restful which we are thus using and enjoying!

We live in a dimension where the racing atom in its minuteness and the speeding constellations in their distant vastness appear to have no effect on us by their motion or timetable, though actually those atoms are the submerged building blocks of our universe. Can we see, therefore, by this analogy, how in a world-to-come where time is no more, where in some manner inconceivable to our minds, past, present and future are simultaneous, where "a thousand years are as one day", what we now regard as the busy activities of daily life may be as motionless rest to us, just as the whirling atoms only produce sensations of solidity and restfulness to us in our present material world? Do we not already have a foreshadowing of this rest which submerges motion in the way that those who know now how to abide in Christ experience a rest which overflows all the pressures and activities of daily life? "For My yoke is easy, and My burden is light."

The second consideration which might help to expand our consciousness is more of a speculation, but we seem to have good grounds for it. We pointed out that the three dimensions of space, the only three conceivable to us, are length, breadth and height. We shewed how the three together, forming our third dimension, are built in increasing ascendancy one upon the other. That is to say, the first dimension is the straight line, which itself is formed by an infinite number of points. If we could conceive of a being living in that dimension, he could not understand or grasp anything outside that straight line. Supposing a square or a cube crossed that line, he would be unable to conceive of such objects, and it would erroneously appear to him only as if some dot had intersected his line. The rest would be unknown to him.

The second dimension, then, would be a combination of length and breadth; and that would mean that an infinite number of straight lines expanded in breadth side by side would form a flat square or a plane. Height would be unknown to a being in that dimension, therefore if a cube intersected with the square, it would appear just as another flat surface at the intersection; the fact of it being a cube with height to it would be incomprehensible. And so in the third dimension, where there is length, breadth and height, where we live. The cube is made up of an infinite number of plane surfaces, one on top of the other; but we can conceive nothing beyond these three dimensions.

Now for a fourth dimension. If there is such, though inconceivable to us, it must consist of an infinite number of cubes, solid bodies, forming some transcendent unit. But is this not just what is shadowed out to us in the Scriptures? All the redeemed being members of *One*—Christ: all things gathered together in *one*—in Christ: the kingdom "delivered up to God, even the Father . . . that God may be *all in all*": time no more, but past, present and future *one*—in Him who is "the first and the last". Is this not an indication that our whole material universe is in some way the building blocks of the new reality, just as points build straight lines for the first dimension, straight lines build planes for the second, and planes build cubes for the third? So cubes, all solid objects of all sizes, will build the fourth dimension, and we who are, by infinite grace, made part of that One Christ will in some way contain *in* us the whole material universe, be in all parts of it at the same moment, with all hearing and all seeing, and all past, present and future: we in Him and He in us, all will be the dimension of eternal life and love.

Now to link that up with our present ministry of prayer. We said that we believed God's people needed a fresh approach to prayer. Do we see why? Prayer is not some poor earth denizens reaching up to some distant Father in some remote heaven, very uncertain about the answers they will get, taking many a shot in the dark, not even always sure if their prayers reach above the ceiling. But get this other concept. God's people are already a new organism, the Tree of life, which is Vine and branches, the "perfect Man", who is Head and body. Human language cannot portray the actual relationship, because it is beyond human understanding. The nearest the Bible can use is the "in" statements: "Ye in Me, and I in you": we in Christ, He in us. These thus carefully preserve the fact that neither Christ nor we lose our distinct identity through eternity, He God, we man; it is never a relationship of total absorption where man ceases to be redeemed man, or Christ ceases to be God the Son. Yet at the same time these "in" statements can obscure from us the actual organic fact, which is also eternally true, of Christ and us having become one "heavenly Man", and in that sense one Christ. We have already referred to such Scriptures as Eph. 4:13; 1 Cor. 12:12; 1 Cor. 6:17; and the identification implied in the word of the Ascended Christ when he charges Paul, the persecutor of the church, with persecuting *Him* (Acts 26:14). It is this latter fact of our organic identification with Him as one new Man which gives us our true orientation for the prayer life. We are actually part of a Christ who, having completed what was necessary for our salvation in His death and resurrection, is now "set down at the right hand of the Majesty in the heavens". We are with Him there, of course, "seated with Him in heavenly places".

Why, and what does that mean? The literal translation of the phrase "in heavenly places" is merely "in the heavenlies", or "in heavenly things" — just the one word in the Greek. We stress that, because we have to get away from the idea that in some mysterious manner we are whisked away in spirit to some distant heavenly realm which is not very realistic for us down here. The truth is that "the heavenlies" are everywhere, only hidden from the natural eye, for God is everywhere. Therefore this reigning Christ ("far above all principalities and powers" of evil) of whom we are a part, is the enthroned Christ just where we are, in ourselves, in our circumstances, in our situations of need and apparent satanic mastery. And why does He thus reign and we with Him? Because He is wholly occupied, in the person of His Spirit, in making His saving grace now known to the world by the members of His body—ourselves—and in "adding to the church daily such as should be saved", and "always causing us to triumph" in Himself, as He makes manifest by us "the savour of His knowledge in every place . . . in them that are saved and in them that perish". There is our praying ground. Not as suppliants in the sense of great distance from Him, of separation from Him, of uncertainty of His will and of a liberal answer; but prayer is seen to be a sharing of His mind on a situation, and our tongues being His mouthpiece in speaking the word of faith.

We are plainly told in Rom. 8:26, 27 that prayer issues from God *in* our hearts, and not just *from* our hearts. It is He praying in us. He tells us what to pray for in our ignorance, which means that we have no business to remain ignorant. The verse says, "the Spirit Himself maketh intercession for us", just because "we know not what to pray for as we ought"; and that does not mean that He is praying for our personal needs on our behalf, but that He is inspiring us to pray for the things and people we ought to pray for; we don't know what they are, but He does, and makes these intercessory prayers in and through us "according to the will of God".

But we may still be asking, How does He make us know what are prayers according to the will of God? The answer is by what He stirs our hearts to desire and ask. We need not be afraid of our "natural" desires. As we have already said, we are new men in Christ, and no longer the old man. As Christ lives in us, therefore, He is living the exact normal life we are living: it is actually He living it, running the business, doing our job, managing the home, cooking the food, looking after the children, active in our church fellowship. In the course of our lives constant need, problems, challenges, frustrations are arising, and in our hearts are longings for deliverances, guidance, supply, the salvation of others, and so on. Those desires are the groanings of the Spirit in us! Somehow we have got such a religious idea of prayer and approach to God, that we hardly dare think that our normal desires are His desires in us. But that is just what they are. They must be if it is Christ living our normal lives in us. You see we have to get back again and again to this heavenly, this "fourth dimension" reality, that He and we are one person. All falls into place when we get the habit of recognizing this, which the Bible calls the walk of faith.

While we are on this point, we had better also face the inevitable question: but what about the times I do pray, hoping and maybe believing it is the will of God, but don't get what I pray for? Am I short in faith, or what? There are such times, sometimes concerning physical healing, when people have had the most absolute assurance of healing, and have declared it; yet the one prayed for has died, or not been delivered. The answer is: prayer is to a *Person*, faith is in that *Person*. The ultimate of prayer is not that God does a certain thing at a certain time in a certain way. I don't mean by that that we cannot ask Him to do so. In our Mission Headquarters we have for years met each morning, considered together what were our immediate projects of faith in our many foreign or home bases, sorted out what seem to us to be obvious needs which should be supplied—and then we have daily prayed the prayer of *faith*.[1] In general

---

[1] A small publication, *Touching the Invisible*, published by Lutterworth Press, tells this story and explains the underlying principles of faith-in-action.

I must say through the experience of thirty years, God gives a vast amount of what we ask for and largely in the way we ask for it; but sometimes not. Then what? I say again faith is in a *Person*. We believe Him. He is true, though all men are liars. All promises in Him are Yea, and we say our Amen to that! So if the thing does not happen as we asked and believed, we still believe, because we are believing *Him*! We don't say the prayer is not answered. Never! We say it is answered. Wait and see! The perfect Biblical illustration of that is Abraham sacrificing Isaac. Isaac was the son of faith, the son in whom the promises were anchored. How could he sacrifice that one? It was God's supreme test on Abraham, not to prove what was in him, God knew that already; but as an example for all time of what faith really means. Abraham's solution of his dilemma was simple, because his faith was single. He believed *God*—that was all. If God told him to sacrifice Isaac, yet God had also said that the promises would be fulfilled in Isaac, then God will raise him from the dead. And Abraham went and acted in that faith, for he said to his servants, at the foot of the mountain, "Abide ye here with the ass; and I and the lad will go yonder and worship, and *come again unto you.*" Abraham's faith was not in the way God does things, but just in God the Doer. That is the answer to the problem of so-called unanswered prayer.

Back to our point then. Prayer is the product of our union with Christ. He in us is the Pray-er. So that the first need in the prayer life is not to pray, but to relax! Quietly, naturally, recognizing the Real One within us, we sort out what warms or stirs our heart with a sense of definite need or challenge. Now we are ready to pray.

What form is our prayer to take? Supplication? Importunity? One fact seems to me to stand out from the lives of the men of the Bible. However they might start their praying, it must end up in faith. It must be the prayer of faith. Indeed they are all called men of faith, rather than prayer, in the Hebrews 11 survey, though it is true that their exploits of faith, when studied in detail, have a background of travail in prayer. And what is significant about their contacts with God? Invariably, as they meet with Him, He tells them that He has something already in hand which He is now going to manifest through them. For Abraham there is God's fixed assurance that he would become a great nation. For Moses there is the sure word that God is going to bring the people out of Egypt and into Canaan, and that he can go before Pharaoh and through the trials in the wilderness in that certainty. For Joshua it is the same; the crossing of the Jordan, the capture of Jericho are declared to him as settled facts well before they took place. And so through all Biblical history. The Saviour Himself knew all about His death and resurrection long before they came to pass, and kept telling His incredulous disciples. What then do all these evidences indicate? That in God's sight these future events were already in existence in His timeless dimension.

It takes us to what we were examining concerning our three dimensions, and the fourth, and to the reason for examining it. And if there is no time with God, and the Bible says there is not: if past-present-future are a permanent and present reality to Him: if the many statements of Scripture on election and predestination, the many prophecies, the many declarations of coming events as already in existence, cover the whole of human history, then it is plain proof, at least to me, that what is true of large events is equally true of small. We too with God may "call the things that be not as though they were", because they really are. How do we do this? Well, personally, as this one or that one, or this or that situation, is on my mind, and I can regard it as within the compass of the interests which are my concern, I straightaway take it for granted that this is a thing already in existence in the invisible. I affirm it as so, I thank the Lord; and as the need, still unsupplied in the visible, keeps returning to my mind, I keep affirming and praising, and stating the fact when it is the right occasion to do so. If my concern is for a fellow-believer, then I keep remembering that, if God has predestinated all believers to be conformed to the image of His Son, He will infallibly do what He says, and by faith I can keep seeing Him in that one, completing what He has begun.

On that same basis, as a missionary secretary, when God has gone out to a mission field in the bodies of some of His servants, I already see the church of Christ in existence among the nationals, where there is nothing visible as yet—and keep seeing it. The same, of course, when some do receive Christ and the young churches begin; I see by faith a complete Christ in them, leading them into the life where God going out through them in serving, saving love is the only reason for their existence. If it is unsaved people, then if they have been brought into my personal circle of concern, I take their salvation as an accomplished fact and that God is in process (it may be through me) of bringing them to Himself. The same with circumstances of need. The negative (not-have) condition is, in the timelessness of God, only the foreshadowing of its dialectical opposite, the positive (the supply). The two are linked, just as it was said that the fallen Adam was only a figure, or foreshadowing, of "Him that was to come"; and in God's eternal outlook, the positive (the last Adam, the Saviour) was in existence and foreordained long before the first Adam was created and fell. So God "saw" the barren Sarah as the mother of nations; and Jesus, for the joy set before Him, endured the cross.

So there it is. We are introduced by the eye of faith into another dimension, a world-to-come, where there is a dissolution in our consciousness, by the authority of the Word of God, of illusory separation; and some scientific discoveries of our day can help rid us of our inhibiting materialistic outlook, and to glimpse both through the Scriptures and by scientific hypothesis our union with a timeless God; and that means the outworking, through the operations of His faith in us, of His purposes which in His sight are already in existence, and a faint foreshadowing of the ultimate glory in our oneness in a one Christ in whom the whole universe will be one in us.

So learn to *release* your burdens, not carry them. Prayer itself may often be unbelief, for instead of glorying in a God who has already done in the invisible what is not yet apparent in the visible, we are nagging at Him to do it! Many a time we are so burdened and occupied in hopelessly hoping for an answer to a prayer we have not really believed, that we have no freedom or largeness of heart to encompass the burdens of others or of a world. A wife can set her husband's salvation back by her "burden" for him, often expressed in unwise preaching at him! Whereas, if she releases him to God by the act of deliberate faith, and keeps repeating that act, she will be more occupied in hopefully loving him than in unbelievingly tearing him down. A mother can be so obsessed with the need of her unsaved children, instead of releasing them to God in faith in the accomplished fact, that she has no heart or vision for the thousands of other unsaved mothers' sons. Prayer meetings also are dead affairs when they are merely asking sessions: there is adventure, hope, and life when they are believing sessions, and the faith is corporately, practically and deliberately affirmed.

Chapter Twenty-two

The Summit

Two New Testament letters celebrate the Ascended Christ—Ephesians and Hebrews. Ephesians opens our eyes to what evidently to Paul's eyes had only been progressively opened, for there is no mention of it in the previous letters. This is the consummation of salvation. Not the cross, not the resurrection, but the ascension. The cross cut us off from the union with Satan; the resurrection gave us union with Christ in our personal living; the ascension gives us union with Him in His world Saviourhood. Here is the panorama of history. We stand on Mount Pisgah and view it. We are already out of this world in spirit, and in the heavenlies. See it, says Paul, and may the eyes of your understanding be enlightened.

It starts with God's foreordination. It ends with the final reconciliation of all things. Its marvelous middle term of grace is the formation of the Christ of eternity by the union of many sons with The Son. These many sons are the spoils of His victory, when He challenged their captor to battle on his own territory. He seized them from him and took them with Himself right through death to resurrection and ascension, right through to His throne in the heavenlies. There He reigns, and they with Him in spirit, far above all. But, if the decisive battle has been fought, the war has not yet been won. The enemy, though defeated, is not yet destroyed. That day will come. Meanwhile, the Son with the sons, the Son in the sons, press home their victory. With spirits in heaven, but bodies on earth, they go to release other captives, millions of them. They go as one army, they keep their own equipment clean and weapons loaded, they endure the hazards and hardships of war. But they don't forget. They have seen the coming end. The shout of a king is among them. One day it will finish, and the hidden throne which they share in spirit will be the universal throne of grace and love; and they will be the body through which the Glorified Head will exercise His eternal ministry of loving service in the universe.

This is Paul's triumph song for the church. A throne shared now. A throne in spirit, while the body that contains it bears the scars of war. It is Christ's throne. See the amazing power which lifted Him from the grave to the right hand of God in actual historic fact, both body and spirit. Believe that the same power has lifted us to the same exalted place in actual spiritual fact, though not yet in our bodies. Then act, not as if this was a glorified experience still to come, not as if this is some mystical throne we are told we share millions of miles away, but as a throne shared down where we are in our own spirits, and in our own defiant world. Actually the enthroned Christ is everywhere: His throne, His lordship, His accomplished victory is in every square inch of the universe. Did He not say, "Go . . . teach all nations . . . and lo,

I am with you always..."? And it is not the resurrected Christ, but the enthroned Christ who is with and in us. Let us get the habit of recognizing this.

I have found it the key to all situations, just when they are difficult, when all seems against deliverance, when the knots of disagreements seem beyond untying, to recognize Christ actually in the situation reigning there, and to take it for granted with thankfulness that we shall see that He is reigning. I learn to enjoy the anticipation of it, and to pray not in needy supplication for a victory, but taking it for granted that the victory is already ours, and to relax.

It is noteworthy that, at the end of his letter, when Paul is making plain that though the great campaign was won, the war is not yet ended and the enemy is rampaging around, he warns us straightly of the mighty power and subtlety of this enemy, and that we "wrestle" with him, and not with the human agents he uses. But then note how he tells us to wrestle. Surely we would think with much fierce striving. But not so. It is again one of those paradoxes of Scripture. We are to wrestle by standing still! For the point of spiritual wrestling is not some form of soulish or physical activity, but the continued wearing of the right armour; and when we look into that list of accoutrements we find they are all varied representations of Christ living in us! Truth round the loins, righteousness for a breast plate, feet shod with the gospel of peace, shield of faith, helmet of salvation, sword of Spirit: in other words, Stand in Christ our truth, righteousness, faith, salvation. As we sit with the Ascended Christ indicating that the victory has been won, so we also walk with Him reigning in life by Him in our daily lives, and stand with Him armed with the weapons of His conquest against a conquered foe.

When we turn from the Ascended Christ in Ephesians to Him in Hebrews, we find a concentration on Him in His office as High Priest rather than on the fact of His enthronement. Nothing is said in actual words about our enthroned relationship with Him. But I suggest that to the eye that can see it, a relationship is etched in, so sensitive and profound that it fully rounds out the high priestly ministry of the enthroned Saviour, and our relationship to Him in it. It actually carries us on beyond the Ephesian revelation to the fullness of the significance of the ascension.

The ostensible objective of the letter, written perhaps by Apollos who was so signally gifted as a teacher of the Word, was the declared purpose of all his teaching, in Acts 18:28, to "shew by the (Old Testament) Scriptures that Jesus is the Christ." This he did in masterly and glorious fashion. Nothing in the Bible surpasses this letter in magnifying Him. As we read it, we can hear the voice that said to Moses, "Put off thy shoes from off thy feet, for the place whereon thou standest is holy ground." The writer had the clear grasp of a Jew upon the centrality of the office of the High Priest in Israel's national life; and he set out to shew that what God had revealed to Moses on the Mount was but the earthly pattern of the heavenly reality. And with what completeness he did it!

He did not start here, however. He began by drawing back the curtain, as it were, on the scene in heaven when the Conqueror returned and was seated in triumph at "the right hand of the Majesty on high".

We shall never be able to do more than imagine that scene. The eternal Son, who had laid aside His equality with God, to be man's Saviour, returning now as the scarred Man in the glory, acclaimed by His Father and worshipped by the angels. "Thy throne, O God, is forever and ever.... Sit Thou on My right hand, until I make Thine enemies Thy footstool.... Let all the angels of God worship Him".

His Saviourhood preceded His high priesthood. A nation must be born of Him over which He will be high priest forever: and saviourhood and high priesthood mean identification. The Son of God becomes the Son of man, and remains man forever. What a revelation! Man in the depths, Man in the heights: Man dying, Man reigning. A saviour must go where the people are to be saved: a high priest must be one of those whom he represents. The Son became Jesus, flesh and blood with flesh and blood, brother among brethren, the Son among many sons. Are they sorely tried? So is He. Do they die in fear? So He drinks that bitter cup to the dregs. Are they tangled in the underbrush of the devil? He goes in front, cutting a pioneer path to freedom. Hallelujah, what a Saviour! And He who was foremost in suffering, will be foremost in song, as He leads countless multitudes in their praise to God through eternity.

"Listen now", the writer goes on to say to his readers, "Israel had a saviour, indeed two saviours: one brought them out of the land of their bondage, and the other into their land of promise: Moses and Joshua. A greater than these is our Saviour; but we had better be sure that we have experienced the benefits of His salvation, as they did of theirs." At

The Summit

least, they all did of Moses, but much fewer of Joshua. They all came out triumphantly enough from under Pharaoh's yoke: "they were all baptized unto Moses in the cloud and in the sea". That is what we would call a regenerating experience, separated from the world, justified by the blood, dead and risen with Christ. But then trouble began. Through ignorance and wilfulness they allowed civil war to rage in their hearts. On the one hand they had the bread from heaven and the water from the rock, which Paul said was Christ to them. On the other, they were constantly racked by fear, unbelief, resentment, murmuring, and even hankerings after the old life in Egypt. They did not know the secret of victory, as Moses did. They had an undiscovered self-life, which God had exposed and dealt with in Moses long before, in the backside of the desert. They foolishly thought that they could be true to God in their own strength; they even replied to God, when He told them how gracious He would be to them if they obeyed Him, "All that the Lord hath spoken we will do". What abysmal self-deception! And all their miserable failures did not open their eyes. So they never entered that land of promise, land of corn and wine, with rest from their enemies. They never made real in their experience the fullness of the blessing which was theirs from the time they joined themselves to Moses, if they had only gone through with him in faith. They died, in the wilderness, not damned souls, but defeated Christians, as we would say.

What about us? the writer asks. We have gone through in faith with our Moses to separation, justification, regeneration, which in fact means death and resurrection with Christ. But then we have landed where the Israelites did in "the waste and howling wilderness" of trial, assaults from the enemy, dryness of soul, good resolutions which we fail to keep. We too have had to learn the hard way that self-effort, though it is the new self, can't keep the commands of God or live the victorious life. Have we learned this? Or do we continue rebellious, resentful, unbroken, like the children of Israel? Do we die in the wilderness, as they, instead of reaching the promised land?

Joshua led a new generation into the land of promise, but it was only a type of the true land of rest. Our Jesus is the true Joshua, and He has provided the true rest: "Take my yoke upon you and learn of Me," He said, "for I am meek and lowly in heart: and ye shall find rest unto your souls". That second rest of Matthew 11:29 is, as we have already seen, the rest of "ceasing from our own works, as God did from His". It is entering in by experience into the actual reality of the old man crucified with Him, and the new man His dwelling place; so that He lives the life in us, not we. We are to exert ourselves and strive diligently to enter in, the Hebrews writer says, and that means take the stand of faith, and continue taking it, until His Spirit bears witness with our spirit that we *are* in the land.

And now, by chapter 5 of this Hebrews letter, we are ready to understand and share in the heavenly ministry of our great High Priest. These early experiences of union with Christ our Moses and Christ our Joshua are spiritual infancy and adolescence, as John explains to us in his epistle (2:12-14). They are designed to release us from the sin and self-life which binds us to earth. They are His cross and resurrection in operation in us. Now we mount up with wings as eagles to the ascended life. But he stops for a moment here. "You can see the earthly side of our High Priest", he says, "made a man among men so as to be 'one of us': and that a high priest is a divine calling, not of man. But I want to tell you that the calling of our Great High Priest is a heavenly and eternal one, and I don't believe you are in the spiritual condition to take it. You can understand the high priesthood of Aaron in an earthly nation, but this is the high priesthood of a Melchisedek over a heavenly nation".

He warns them in great seriousness, as Paul wrote to the Galatians: "I am alarmed about you . . . I stand in doubt of you". They were God's redeemed people, "holy brethren" he called them; but instead of pressing on and through to God's full salvation, entering into His rest, they were stopping short, like Israel in the wilderness. Having got into clear water themselves, they should be piloting others; but instead, they were needing reminders of the elementaries of the gospel. They were in dangerous waters; for there is no standing still in the river of God. There were turbulent rapids ahead, and the barque of their faith could be capsized, and they drowned. This was no light matter, no question of sins of the daily life into which we all so easily fall, but take the way of quick repentance to where we find the mercies of God awaiting us. This was the dangerous drift, the backsliding of neglect which hardens into apostasy, until we actually trample under foot the One at whose feet we were formerly prostrate, regard as valueless the blood which was once most precious, and turn a contemptuous back on the Spirit who first wooed and won us to the grace of God: and we reach the point of no return. The writer does not mince matters, and piles warning on warning through the letter. There are only two ways for the believer, either forward to perfection, or back to apostasy. The storms of life blow fiercely, those to whom he was writing were feeling their icy blast: persecution, deprivation, exile, torture, death. Who could withstand their fury? Certainly not unsanctified self: only the Christ within. And we may well ask ourselves, who read this to-day: How would we stand them? The answer is the same. We could not: but Christ in a redeemed self makes us more than conquerors. Paul could endure all things, because he could "do all things through Christ which strengtheneth me".

To these "wrestlers with the troubled sea", however, he did reach out the hand. "We have an anchor," he wrote; "hold fast to it! It has two arms which are securely grounded where nothing can move them—'within the veil'. They are the promise and oath of God. What could be stronger than they? It was by clinging to them that Abraham persevered until he obtained. You do the same. Follow through with them, and you will find within that same veil the eternal, heavenly high priest of whom we are speaking."

But the point of his warning and hesitation concerning their ability to comprehend what he now wanted to reveal about the heavenly High Priest was that, while we believers are still immersed in fighting our personal battles or oppressed by our own tribulations, we are not free in mind and heart to enter into the world purposes, the world responsibilities, and the price that must be paid, to be priests along with the Great High Priest, and to apprehend the meaning and greatness of the calling. For this, we must have gone through with our Moses and Joshua into the promised land of rest from our own works and concerns, and be living in that land.

Either the Bible is the inspired record of God's word, or it is not; for the two chief evidences from the Old Testament of the foreordination of Christ as our Saviour on earth and High Priest in heaven are just two sentences, and one of these depends upon the difference of one letter! Paul bases his proof that the plan of God in sending the Saviour was confined to the one line of faith, by quoting God's word to Abraham that the promise would be fulfilled not through "seeds, as of many; but as of one, And to thy seed, which is Christ". The writer to the Hebrews traces back the appointment of Christ to be the eternal High Priest to the one inspired statement through the mouth of David, spoken once and never repeated, "The Lord hath sworn, and will not repent, Thou art a priest forever after the order of Melchizedek".

The Old Testament type of the everlasting priesthood, the real high priesthood, was not the much publicized, historic office first held by Aaron, but the obscure entrance and disappearance from history of the king-priest with whom Abraham had dealings, and to which reference is only once made! It took the inner eye of revelation in the Hebrews writer to bring out the glories and implications of that mysterious figure; and incidentally it shews how much is wrapped up in statements and incidents of the Bible which only the enlightened can interpret.

This is our heavenly High Priest, holding no office

on earth, and a heavenly High Priest must represent a heavenly people. So, by centering on Him, passed through the heavens, made higher than the heavens, seated at the right hand of the Majesty on high, by implication the writer is saying that we too are there; for a high priest is always one of, among, and acting for his people. His objective in these next chapters is to transfer our faith and attention, once for all, to our true nationality, homeland, royal lineage, and palace privileges, and the effects such have on our daily life.

Here He stands, replacing the earthly makeshifts of mortal priests, ineffectual law, inconclusive sacrifices. See Him, eternal in His appointment, unchangeable in His ministry, irreproachable in His character. God's oath established Him: the power of an endless life sustains Him: a completed sacrifice crowns His advocacy. Limitless salvation for His people, nothing less, are the crown rights of such a limitless Intercessor.

What is the first of these crown rights? An everlasting covenant, with no conditions attached. The former covenant was dependent on human obedience. Hopeless condition. Like all the rest of the law, with its demand on man, it was "weak through the flesh". The new covenant is briefly defined in the language of the Old Testament prophets as the writing of God's Law in our hearts, and all knowing Him. In New Testament language we can interpret that simply enough as "Christ in you, the hope of glory", this inner union being based, again using the language of the prophets, on "their sins and their iniquities will I remember no more"—justification by faith. The covenant is "the grace of God which bringeth salvation" in its completeness.

If the first crown right (ch. 8) is God's full salvation, the second crown right (ch. 9) is its continued maintenance by a continual cleansing. This is the High Priest who has entered once for all into the holy place with His own blood, the blood of sprinkling which is spoken of as eternally present in Mount Zion (12:24), "speaking better things than that of Abel". This is the High Priest in His office as Advocate with the Father, the propitiation for our sins, when we sin. This is the continued cleansing of the conscience in His blood, when we are convicted of the sins of self-effort (dead works), continuously liberating us for the service of the living God. This, we believe, is the correct interpretation of the intercessory work of our High Priest, so far as our needs of daily cleansing are concerned. Not that we are to think of Him daily bending the knee as suppliant to the Father for us, but rather seated at His right hand, the wounds in His hands and feet (the Lamb as it had been slain) bearing permanent witness to the eternal redemption His blood purchased for us, and therefore unending forgiveness of sins and cleansing from all unrighteousness.

The third crown right (ch. 10) is the sanctification, separation and dedication of all redeemed human personalities for their predestined end. By the offering up of His body, our bodies have become His purchased possession. "For their sakes I sanctify myself (set myself apart), that they also might be sanctified (set apart)". We are the earthen vessels. We are the temples. We are the branches. We are the body. Wholly released by the blood of Christ for our sins, and by the body of Christ for our sanctification, we are instruments meet for the Master's eternal use, prepared unto every good work.

The heavenly High Priest has His heavenly people, the kingdom of priests with the Royal Priest, eternally joined to Him by the covenant of union, eternally cleansed by His blood, eternally dedicated to their true destiny.

What is that destiny? It is quietly slipped in the great eleventh chapter. The writer had warned them that he didn't know whether they could catch the meaning of the heavenly priesthood. So he presents us with the Great High Priest, His entrance into heaven, His enthronement in heaven, His intercessory work for all who come to God by Him, based on the totality of His atonement. And there the record seems to stop. We seem left with Him there, disconnected from us except by the approaches of faith. It seems a static situation rather than dynamic, except for the exhortations to us to hold fast to the end. The real meaning of it all lies concealed except for those who have eyes to see. It is the method of "indirect communication" by which truth is there for those who can find it, but it cannot be pressed on to any, for it must be inwardly embraced. It is like Jesus so often saying, "He that hath ears to hear, let him hear", and the cause of Him so often clothing truth in parables whose meaning could be unfolded only to the initiated.

The secret is the High Priest, to whom the royal priesthood of the redeemed are joined as body to Head, moving back into the world in saving activity through us, the priests. Hebrews eleven is the great list of those through history by whom He has been fulfilling His intercessory work in the world. In other words, the High Priest fulfills part of His ministry as intercessor for the body in the presence of God by being our advocate with the Father, being Himself the propitiation for our sins through His blood. He fulfills another part by returning to the world in the person of the Spirit, to dwell in His body and preserve them blameless until His coming, thus saving them to the uttermost. He fulfills yet another part by reaching out to save the world through His body, they now being royal priests through whom the Priest-King continues His intercessory work for a lost world. He continues His dying and rising through them; they fill up that which is behind of His afflictions; they partake in the fellowship of His sufferings and are made conformable to His death. These men of faith in Hebrews eleven were not just a glorious company of martyrs; they were Christ's saving agents in each generation—Noah, Abraham, Moses, David, the prophets, the apostles, right up to every member of the body of Christ. They lived with a purpose. Each could say, as Jesus Himself when on earth, "To this end was I born, and for this cause came I into the world, that I should bear witness unto the truth."

Now the ascended Christ, the Great High Priest, is seen as the dynamic Saviour doing His saving work, as much as ever, through His body. Or perhaps it should be said that He was the Saviour once for all in His own body, but now He is the Intercessor in and through our bodies—to gather the spoils of His victory. We may speak of "the heavenlies" as some distant place, the Mount Zion where He and the Father are, with the church of the firstborn, the spirits of just men made perfect, the heavenly Jerusalem, and we locate it way off somewhere. But the Hebrews writer says, "Ye *are* come to Mount Zion, and unto the city of the living God" (12:22); not, "Ye *will* come one day!" We are, therefore, already part of this wonderful heavenly company, and must regard "the heavenlies" as interpenetrating our world, and our Great High Priest occupied in fighting the battles of salvation in this lost world by us.

As our ascended Christ, according to Ephesians, we can always know that we have in us and in our circumstances a reigning Lord, reigning in just this situation; and we can see Him as such by faith, and rejoice. This is how the victors of faith of whom we read in Hebrews eleven walked in their victory, often not outwardly delivered at all, even to death and torture, often living in destitute conditions, though sometimes seeing the manifested fruits of their faith.

As our Great High Priest, according to Hebrews, He shares with us His priesthood. That puts deeply serious purpose into every condition and situation in life. It is not that just a few select people are Christ's royal priesthood (heading up in the horrible error in which some ministers of the gospel reserve for themselves the name of priest). Every member of Christ's body is a member of the royal priesthood. We are what Israel was meant to be, "A kingdom of priests". You and I are part of this "holy priesthood".

Then how does that work out in normal daily living? Like this. A priest is an intercessor. An intercessor is one who recognizes that he is set apart by God to stand in some gap against the enemy of souls (Ezek. 22:30). How and where? Just exactly where you are. Open your eyes so that God is looking through them at your situation, and you will surely see your commission; for all life is a commission for those who can see it.

Then accept the commission. That will be bearing about in your body the dying of the Lord Jesus, because it may well go against your human grain to accept it. You may have a real battle to do so. The way to fight and win is to recognize that it is He and none else who is living just there in you, and put you there, and brought to you the pressure and burdens which form your present environment. Accept it, even though you feel the opposite and continue to feel it. You are now consciously in the privileged position of being an intercessor, a royal priest.

But an intercessor does more than accept a situation. He accepts the fact that he is specifically God's agent in it, and that God has put him there because He is going to do something definite through him. So an intercessor is not a vague drifter, just passively yielding to some difficult situation. He is a person with a purpose, because the purposing Christ is within him. The next stage, then, is the challenging one. An intercessor, so far as he is given to do so, takes the place of those for whom he intercedes, even as Jesus took our place. Jesus went all the way we go right to death, and "through death destroyed him who has the power of death"; that is to say, He bore all we bear, but He bore it in faith, whereas we natural humans bear it in despair. Now we are to be as Jesus, Jesus in us, in our places of intercession. We are to bear people's unpleasantness, their sharp tongues, their taunting of us as hypocrites, their selfishness, their overreaching us. How can we do that? We shall feel it certainly; but as we put ourselves in their place, we think more of their inner miseries in such a condition than of the hurt they do us; that is what it means to turn the other cheek, and as God gives grace, we shall bear with them and keep loving them. There may be plenty of cost in this, and it may last—a lifetime? Think of a foreign missionary and the years of patience it takes with a prejudiced, unresponsive people. But the point is that it is a life with a purpose. We know what we are doing when we are intercessors. We have an objective in view, and we pay any price God gives us to pay to obtain it. "Who, for the joy set before Him, endured the cross . . . ."

With the direct commission, with the acceptance of it, and with the price being paid, there is the authority of faith. We have already talked of this. It means that, if God appointed us to this situation, and the situation to us, then God's purpose of grace will be fulfilled; indeed in the sight of Him who "calleth the things that be not as though they were" it has already been fulfilled, and was fulfilled before the situation arose—the supply before the need. We persist, then, in the affirmation and expectation of faith. "Abide ye here with the ass; and I and the lad will go yonder and worship, and *come again to you.*" So said Abraham to his servant when he left him at the foot of the mountain and took Isaac up to sacrifice him.

Priesthood and the intercession which is the ministry of the priest is the topmost pinnacle of God's ways with us. We have come full circle. God is love. Love is pure self-giving. By the sacrifice of Himself He has won back to Himself millions who had become His enemies. Living in them, He now loves through them. Love is pure self-giving. We now give ourselves that millions more may find Him. When they do come to Him, He lives in them as in us. Love is pure self-giving. They now love with the love of God. And so the eternal stream of God flows on.

Chapter Twenty-three

From Lowlands to Highlands in a Series of Letters

A series of letters from a friend of my wife and myself, a lady living in a difficult situation with her husband and four children, will illustrate in a personal way what I have been saying and will, I believe, bring this book to a right ending. Often plain down-to-earth heart outpourings will illuminate as theory never will. I have extracted, with her permission, what I think hits the spot.

The letters start with her desperate search for light:

"July 13, 1957. Tell me, Mr. Grubb, what does it mean to be 'in Christ'? That has bothered me for five years. One does not get that in church—just how to be born again, support their program, read your Bible and you will grow in grace. I know it means union, vine and branch, out of Adam into Christ, representation, identification. I've come to the conclusion that it is the key to the New Testament, and all my studying of it has made it more a mystery. There is a veil over my eyes that only the Holy Spirit can take away. I know that I was chosen in Christ before the foundation of the world, before Adam and Eve were born, before Christ came in the flesh, before I came in the flesh, before I accepted Him. Now I am in Him visibly. God called those things which be not as though they were; and then they came into being, and some things took quite a time to come about in the visible. Now does it work the same way in taking the faith position? The Father counts us dead when Christ died, and us resurrected when Christ resurrected: so when I take what my Father has declared, then what was not becomes? So what was always in the invisible comes to be in the visible? I do wish that you would ask God to take my graveclothes off and keep my resurrected ones on. I also want the Holy Spirit. I know what I have been taught about the Holy Spirit, but I believe the way Moody, Torrey, and Studd believed. I want the Holy Spirit and I want Him on His own terms.

"July 16. I thought that God would prosper us, we would tithe and teach Sunday School, raise the children as Christians. That was really living. All I knew was to teach how to be born again and to surrender, that was all I had been taught. But that is not enough, and difficult circumstances and people showed me that it was not.

This last situation also brought things to a head. I discovered there was an ego within that wanted to be independent of God. I did not know it was there. I could usually always get out of situations or I could go to work to pay bills. But this was one which I could do nothing about. I saw that we were made to be dependent. I also saw that it was God that had always delivered in the past. I also saw the necessity of the wilderness experience to get at that pride. I had been brought up in a home, and I was determined that I could always take care of myself. Yes, I trusted God, but I now see I trusted self more. Yes, I was consecrated, but that is not enough. Sin was always cropping out. I told the Lord it was like having a floor full of eggs, and when trying to avoid one, you stepped on ten. One tried to control one sin, and it cropped out in ten places. Read the Bible? I even have it on records which I played morning to night. Did they sanctify me? No, I confessed sin from morning to night. Did I try? Yes, but the more I tried, the more I sinned. The first time I heard that I had been crucified with Christ and to reckon myself dead to sin and alive to God, it was telling me white was black and black was white and I was to agree to it. But I *am* beginning to see that we are to call things as our Father calls them, and judge not by appearances, but judge righteous judgment.

"Oct. 17, 1957. Would you ask Him to open my blind eyes that I may know what it means to be *in Christ and Christ in me*? I have studied and I have read everything that I can on the subject of the union with Christ. I have read Law, Boehme, Murray, Ruth Paxson's *Life on the Highest Plane,* holiness literature, Pentecostal, flesh versus spirit, Darby and Ironside (I believe these have done more damage to victorious living than any I know), Newell's book on Romans, Gordon's *In Christ*, Pierson's *In Christ Jesus*, Jukes, Keswick teaching. I believe that God will not do for a person what they can do themselves, and I have studied, studied, and studied until my brain is foggy. I have gone my limit, and I believe that only the Holy Spirit can enlighten me. I have got to know what it means to be in Christ. To me it is the key to the whole New Testament. Oh, I could write a thesis on it and speak about it, but I honestly do not know. No explanation has satisfied me. I see and I do not see. It is tied up in two creations—in Adam and in Christ, and it is the key to representation and identification. Brother Grubb, would you forget that I am a woman of thirty-five and explain it to me as you would to a little child? I believe that people would enter in if they understood. The words, 'My people perish because of lack of knowledge', burn within me, and I believe that with all my heart. I believe that one must understand what it means to be *in Christ*, before one can reckon oneself dead to sin and alive unto God in Christ Jesus, because the visible is sure to come up, and unless you understand, your faith will go down.

I can't even solve my own problems, and my independent ego always gets in the way. I'm just plain dumb and ignorant, but surely God has made a place for the dumb, for He made me. The same God that made the eagle made the ant, and He has a place for both and both are necessary. How one can be so thirsty, when the water of life is within, so hungry when the bread of life is within, so weak and dumb when the great I AM is within who has all power, all wisdom, and strength, I don't know.

Mr. L. said we had the old nature, and when Christ came in, we had two natures. One would always sin, and of course that allowed you to act like a child of the devil, and then you could always claim forgiveness through the blood. I said I once believed that, and what confusion it put me in, for I did not know who was who inside of me—the old man, the new man, the flesh, sin, and Christ; and what misery it constantly put me in. I am beginning to see the damage the theory of the two natures does, and that it is the big lie of the serpent. By the theory of the two natures, one has standing and state, and your standing is never your state, and gives you the excuse to sin. This theory only knows an historical Christ and can see Christ on every page of the Bible, but it will never expose the independent ego.

As yet, I know that of myself I can do nothing and am nothing, but I honestly do not know that union with Christ. Oh, to know that union with Christ, where Christ is the all and I just the container, Christ the vine and I the branch, Christ the head and I the body, Christ the water and I the vessel. In my mind I have separated the inseparable. Christ the head in heaven, and I here on earth the body. Christ the vine in heaven, and I the branch on earth, etc. Brother Grubb, can you help me?"

The realization then came. Faith was the victory. Her letters take on a new note:

"Nov. 30. The light is beginning to dawn that Christ is within me, and just count on Him being there at all times, and He will manifest Himself through me. The word of the Lord comes; then you must declare what the Lord says; then the visible looks like the exact opposite, and that is the reason for being strong and courageous; then the word of the Lord tries you, but just take God at His word and thank Him for answering; and then, as night follows day, the invisible is made visible.

"Dec. 15. I have finally seen that scheming self cannot do it, even consecrated self. In this warfare with Satan self is powerless and only the Holy Spirit can war against him successfully. I have finally seen at last that we are absolutely helpless and made to be completely dependent upon God, and God will deliver when we give up trying to help Him. God will not share His glory with another. He will not spare us.

"Jan. 3, 1958. I have finally seen the *fact* that I have been crucified with Him and I maintain it by faith, but as yet He has not given me the realization of possession; but I know that in His own way and time He will do so. Before, I was trying to possess by faith what I did not know as fact. It was in Romans 5 that I saw the truth of it—of the one acting for all—the first Adam and then the Second Adam. For the past 14 years I have desired to see this truth, and particularly the last 7 years where the desire has mounted up so that I find myself even dreaming of these things.

"Feb. 18. For 17 months this has been a fight in the heavenly places and I have had to do with evil spirits. For 17 months there have been few days that I have not been on my face before the Lord, and my Bible and bedroom floor is stained with tears. Perhaps if I had known then of my union with Christ, it would not have been necessary. I likened myself to hanging on to the Rock with the gales blowing so strong that I have had to hold on for fear of being blown off by the storms, not realizing that I was part of the Rock, eternally joined. But when I told the Lord the burdens were too much, the Spirit asked me how industry tested new articles, and the inevitable answer was that new articles are always tested 5 to 10 times their normal use, and the things of the Spirit can be put to the same test."

Freed from herself, she begins to move out from

herself to the wonder of Christ living in her, and to see and discuss some of the laws of the life in the Spirit.

"March 23. I have caught a glimpse of why you ignore the devil. There are two realms. There is the realm of resisting and getting into conflict; but there is also the higher which is above all—Christ enthroned within and without. The light is beginning to shine and the darkness is going. I am seeing the various laws of the Spirit realm contained in the Scriptures, such as resistance and war against the devil versus standing in Christ ignoring the enemy, and fighting the visible circumstances and going under versus looking at Jesus reigning within and without. According to the laws you use, the results will be. God has many laws in the spiritual realm just as there are a lot of laws of electricity. If one does not know the laws of electricity and one starts tampering with electricity, one gets shocked. I got my spiritual laws mixed up, going from one realm to the other, and I got spiritual shocks until an 'electrician' got me centered in Christ and standing in Him, realizing that He reigns within and without and we are in His invisible (but almighty) kingdom now. Love and faith are the weapons of the Holy Spirit, and they utterly destroy the devil and his works. A little more light was shed—we reign in life by Christ Jesus and are kings and priests unto God. Priests do not war, they just intercede and submit to God; kings speak the word of authority and it is done.

I wondered why you did not resist the devil when you prayed with me, and I began meditating and searching. I knew you were using a higher law but I did not understand; for there were those other Scriptures about resisting the devil and about the believer having to do the resisting. But I persisted and I finally saw how darkness goes when the light comes in, and then I saw and understood.

The battle was really between Satan and the Holy Spirit. I now realize what you meant when you said God's blessings are good and the devil's attacks are turned into good. All things work together for good, not just 99, but 99 plus 1. I realize that God gave me a front seat on seeing how darkness works and then how the Light works. The devil—bing, bang, bomb. The Lord works silently and naturally. The devil can go so far, just as the ocean can come on the sand so far. I definitely now see that we do not wrestle against the darkness, but abide in the Light. God will bruise Satan under our feet in His time. I now see that it is God's way of maturing us in Christ. I take it by faith that in years to come I will say these past six months were the best thing that happened to me—to realize the union with Christ.

I now see what you meant by guided praying and gaining a place of intercession. One can't cash in on your experiences or Studd's or Muller's or Blumhardt's. One has to go that way and there is a price. One can only go as Jesus reveals, for He is the Life. I now know what you mean when you say, 'I'll do it when Jesus tells me.' Yes, He speaks within. Amazing grace. How wonderful to realize that the Almighty One, the Creator, the Lamb, dwells in me—the no thing. Yes, just a container for His Life to flow out to others. Two people dwelling as one, joined, yet He thinks His thoughts and I think my thoughts, and two different wills, yet my will just wants to flow with His. Marvelous, marvelous, marvelous grace. Oh, that the world could know it.

On March 31st it will be seven years since I absolutely surrendered to the Lord, and it has all been down hill, and the last six months rock bottom. But it is necessary to get at independent ego. I now know that one can be dependent on God. We ought to know that we can trust God, but we do not really, until God puts us in places where we cannot possibly deliver ourselves, and then He delivers us."

The "rest of faith" was now becoming real to her:

"May 26. I am beginning to realize that since we are in Christ (and it was God who put us there), that finished work of His two thousand years ago covers all situations. Just to stand in Him to me means to *sit down* on His finished work—a ceasing of one's own works and resting on His. It has come very gradually, and I am coming to know that I died with Him, for I was in Him from the time I was born of Him. I believe that a realization that one is in Him must come before one can stand in Him with faith. When the realization comes that one is in Christ and that God put you in Him, there is nothing to do but to cease from one's own works. It is also the difference between trying to gain a victory by works of the flesh, and just resting in Him, realizing that His victory two thousand years ago covered the present distressing situation.

The Holy Spirit opened much more on this line and it is the same in prayer—less praying and more praise; for as I count on His finished work covering the present situation, the faith just rises up and praise follows and thanks are given that you have already received what you asked for.

I am also beginning to realize that Christ lives His life in us. I can't explain how it came about, but I think while out in Missouri, I began to realize that Christ was carrying out His plans in me. It is difficult to put into words. While out in Missouri the Holy Spirit revealed conditions in our country which I had not realized were so very very bad. First, in the rural churches one does not get the A of the Gospel, let alone anything of the crucified life. America has an historical Christ, and He can't profit her anything. All I know is that the Holy Spirit was crying within me for our nation and yearning over the people for whom He died, yearning for those who professed Him but were backslidden, and yearning for those who despised Him. I do not know how to describe it, but I know the Holy Spirit was pouring out His heart in me over His Own and for those who were still out of the fold.

"May 27. I did not get the letter off yesterday and thought you might be interested in knowing that the Lord dealt with self-righteousness. Somewhere in my mind, I had divided the good from the bad in self. I was wanting to keep the good, for I thought it good; but the Lord showed me that the whole had to go to the cross. It was that exposure of self in the innermost part. Self thinks it can live the Christian life until God starts pressing, and then it shows itself for what it is. Just like honey—honey is sweet, but put some fire under it and what a smell. It was an awful shock that all had to go to the cross, and in God's sight it had already gone. I also realize that I was trying to keep the law of God in my own strength, before reckoning myself dead to sin and alive unto God and Christ living within. I was doing it unconsciously and that is why there was no victory. I was trying to make self obey, and self cannot obey the law. There must be a ceasing of one's own efforts and just rest on Christ fulfilling it within. This has only come through defeat after defeat because of being under so much of the two nature theory—state and standing, position and walk. Though they give one the position of being in Christ, sooner or later it crops up that one has to do something to get in. In talking about being strong in the Lord, one writer was saying that in order to be strong, one must be planted in His death before one can be strong in His life. That strikes to the heart of a child of God with Satan on his trail, for it sets that person trying to get in. The fact is that that person is *in Christ and therefore has been planted into his death, and they are strong in the Lord for they are in Him.* The two nature theory will not expose that hidden ego, and also the falsity that reckoning means that it is not really so. But the facts of the Scriptures show us that we are in Christ and His history has become ours, and reckoning is just accounting or appropriating what God has already provided.

Oh, what I was taught was alright while there were no storms, but as soon as the storms of life come, those teachings will not help. I am going to an interdenominational church. It is fundamental of fundamentalism—but it is still the A of the Gospel, and it will not suffice when the storms of life blow. They do not seem to know there is a B and a C of the Gospel. All we have here in America is evangelists and so few Bible teachers in the Scriptural sense of the word."

Writing concerning severe domestic and financial problems:
"June 29. Strangely enough, it does not seem to

bother me since the day before I wrote you in February. During the previous 18 months I pleaded every promise in the Bible, knew all the heart cries of David in the Psalms, pleaded the covenants. I do not know whether this is "rest" I am experiencing, for I do not seem to have a care in the world. The devil tells me I am utterly silly and that I have been brain washed.

About a month ago as I was thinking over the situation, it came to me that I was in exactly the same position a person would be in if there had been gambling. Only God Himself could have arranged such circumstances and He was living His life in me. The same Person who got us in this mess would get us out. I would not begin to try. It was funny to realize that Christ was living His own life in me and carrying on His own purposes in His own way. There was no emotion, just a realization of the fact.

The next day when all hell broke loose, I said (or rather the Spirit of my Father said) the creative words that brought the thing into being. First the thought, then the word, and it came into being. It was not I who brought it into being, but the Father, Son, and Holy Ghost, but *through* me. Again, no emotion, but the realization of a fact that the Triune God is living in me, carrying out His own purposes. That is really quite a revelation to realize that God is really living in one and really living His own life in one of His creatures. That is how God reveals Himself to me. I know nothing of overwhelming power or emotion or God speaking directly to me in a loud voice.

The Lord has been opening up Ephesians in a marvelous way. I've discovered that we are not only born crucified, but born enthroned with the ascended

Christ. Also the heavenlies are not way up there, but are down here. The right hand of God means the center of power of the entire universe. Head and body make One. Wherever a member of the Body is, Christ is, for one could not be a member of the body unless Christ were within.

"July 3. God has been opening up more in Ephesians about the life of sharing the throne with Christ. The key to me is in the first chapter *'to usward who believe.'* It may not hold much to others, but to me it is like an open door of a vast dominion—to us who act in accordance with these facts that we are really delivered out of Satan's authority into the kingdom of His Son and share His authority. I see that God has to use shadows to reveal the invisible which is the real Substance. We tend to hold on to the shadows and thereby miss the Substance.

In meditating in Romans 6 on how the old man is out, the new man helpless in 7 and Christ in us in 8, I was thinking how the illusions are so contrary, just like in physical life. If a person gets his tonsils out, he says his tonsils hurt (how can tonsils hurt if they are out?). If one gets an arm or foot or any other member cut off, the person usually complains that the limb which is cut off hurts him, and he says it until death. Illusions, are they not? When we get cut off in Christ's death with the circumcision not made with hands, we have had quite a severe operation. What illusions we have and quite painful, but they are illusions.

It is a marvelous truth that Christ is living His own life in us. It has come to me just very slowly, but it is a fact and not feeling. I realize that there are those who feel His presence constantly, but He has not been pleased to manifest Himself to me that way. I find that He will manifest Himself through me rather than to me."

Now she begins to see the ultimate meaning of the Christ-in-us life—intercession:

"July 1, 1959. The Lord has been revealing some more laws of intercession or perhaps I am beginning to see some of them more clearly. The Holy Spirit is the intercessor within us, and it is He who makes us one with the person. We do not have anything to do with it at all. When I say He makes us one with the person, it is really He in us making Himself one with the person. He even arranges circumstances to suit Himself. I find that the Holy Ghost identifies Himself in us with the person and He consumes us completely. I did not understand this before.

I am beginning to realize that God has thrown me in amongst sinners to do a saving work of grace. I was beginning to grumble about my lack of fellowship with saints, but the Lord showed me He uses His body to save the lost and is not the slightest interested in our reactions. It is His body and He intends to use it and there is not much room for self when He is living His own life in us, for He is such an outgoing Person and consumes and refuels us for others. When I've complained of having no life of my own to live, He shows me in no uncertain terms there is only one life and He is living His own life the way He wants to in me. The Lord and I have argued over that and it has taken some time to come up to that, and I know He will pull me through, for He always does.

What I am beginning to see is this in intercession. The Holy Spirit needs a clean vessel to intercede in by identification with the ones in need. Then after the identification, He expresses Himself in that human body in groanings of utter agony which are wordless, and then all of a sudden it stops and you know (not reason) that God is going to do something. It seems that He needs a body to feel and live in certain of life's circumstances, but He needs a clean vessel utterly abandoned to Himself to carry this out, and the person He intercedes in is a victim and it is a death, but somehow or other there is life for others out of it. It is not just holding this in theory or doctrine, but a real death. It is something I know in the utter depths within, but vaguely understand. Just as I know that if you plant an apple seed it dies, but up from it comes an apple tree with fruit for all. I know that this is true, but I do not understand it, but I know it is a law, and it just works that way. This is a hard saying for flesh. You can get a hundred people to pray with you for a request, for temporal or even spiritual things; but the only prayers that count are only those in whom they will go all the way with the Spirit. That was quite a shattering blow. He can change us, but we can't change the Eternal One. If a housewife is going to bake a cake, she will use the ingredients on hand. She would not think of going out and buying the ingredients she has on hand, only unless she is out of them. When we give our wills and our bodies to the Spirit and, of course, all our meagre possessions go with it, the Spirit really takes over and begins to use our former will, body, possessions as He purposes. Unlike us, He is completely self-giving and very generous. He loves the ungodly and He in us loves them through us. We ourselves do not love the ungodly, but are used to loving those who love us. He loves those who hate and despise Him, and wants to use our bodies to show forth this love. This is the bitter part of sanctification, until one sees what He is doing. We are used to living the self life, but He in us is pouring through us His Love to the ungodly. It takes a little while to get used to this new life flowing through us to others.

Also, I have seen the difference between deliverance and death. A Christian always has a right to be delivered for he is God's child, but deliverance for myself does not carry with it deliverance for others or change Satan's captives into Christ's captives. Death and through death carries resurrection life for others, and changes Satan's captives into Christ's captives. He delivered us, but He had to take death to do it. The servant is not greater than his master. The choice is ours. Who is going to live the life in us—the redeemed I who can be delivered but can't deliver others, or the Holy Spirit in us who finds Himself in giving Himself? In this union within who is going to *live the life,* Christ or I?

I believe that X has been using the law of resistance in prayer, and I believe that it is affecting her health. I hope that in your new book you show why you do not resist the devil, but defeat him by just abiding in the Light. I had to find the error. By just abiding in the Light one realizes that Christ's victory defeated Satan, and by that victory all present situations have already been won, and one just rests on that fact. Satan's one tactic or wile is to get one out of abiding and to start a fight of resistance. Some teach there is a fight in this realm, and then after the conflict they show you just standing in the Lord—like going up from conflict to standing. But that is the error: we do not go up, for we are already up and the battle has already been won. It takes *faith* just to stand still and do nothing, realizing it has already been won, when all around you looks like the contrary. It takes faith to stand still, resting on an accomplished victory, when outwardly a battle is raging; and even to believe that God can turn the evil into good—the cursing into blessing."

Finally, like a ship loosed from its moorings and out on the eternal seas, like Paul, she "comprehends with all saints what is the breadth, and length, and depth, and height":

"Jan. 18, 1961. It is marvelous to know that Christ is in us, but how much greater to know we who are in Christ are One. The realization of the fact that Christ is in me was wonderful, but the realization of the fact of the entire Oneness of the Body was more glorious. The Holy Spirit gave a simple illustration and brought it down to my level. There are many members of our human body yet one body, and we are only as well or as strong as the weakest member in our human body. If I get a boil, or a virus attacks me and settles in my body, I still do not regard it as part of me, even though it is in me. I regard it as an invader. If I get a boil on my left hand, my right hand will not hit the left hand, but will aid in doing what it can to get it rid of the boil by applying a poultice or whatever else the head suggests. Though it sees the left hand diseased, it does not disregard it as part of the body and it does not condemn the left hand being treated by the right hand; but what about in the invisible parts of our body? There is the mystery: we see corpuscles not condemning but giving up their own life to rid it of the disease, going to the aid of the harmed hand. Our mind sees both the perfection of the body and also the disease; but does not see them equal. It sees and regards the hand perfect, even though it also sees the disease which is minor. Now the Spirit began to teach me, or shall I say I just began absorbing what the Spirit had been teaching all along, but I was too stupid to see. Christ is not only in us, but we are in Him and therefore part of each other. Now since my children had confessed Christ as Saviour, we are part of each other for we are joined to One Spirit which means one Life, not many but One; yet we remain ourselves and He remains Himself. Now I began to see why I could confess the sins of my children and see Christ work. I was only as strong as my weakest child, only as well as my sickest child, for the One Life which flowed in them flowed in me. That opened up a vast domain of thought. I actually got lost in the Spirit, for I started exploring all of these things. As I went about my work, my thoughts were not on what I was doing but, on these wonders of Oneness. Pris would talk to me, and to get my attention she would have to yell before I realized she was talking to me. As far as the body of flesh is concerned, I have been in isolation, but in Spirit I have been all over the universe. In the Spirit there is no such thing as time or space. It is so wonderful, so marvelous and yet so practical.

    I am just beginning to comprehend the greatness and the majesty of our Lord. He is so great and yet He is so common. Sometimes I laugh at Him in some of the experiences or circumstances He puts me in, and sometimes I stand in utter awe of Him. It is just like I am beginning to know Him, and things of earth fade away. Not that I have not wanted to write, but it is hard to put down on paper these things and give understanding. Oh, the depths of the depths of the Spirit, and yet I have touched the fringe of understanding only. Also when I saw the oneness of our each being part of each other in the Body, it made such a difference. Before really seeing this truth, I could see the sins of other believers more clearly than Christ in them. Now I see Christ in them and the sin as the virus. Now when I see sin in a member, I do exactly what I do for myself, and regard them as hating sin as I do. When I sin, I confess it immediately, get the cleansing of the blood, and regard myself as perfect in Christ, having on the white garments of Christ's righteousness. When I see sin in a member, I confess the sin, claim cleansing and see that member perfect in Christ. That sets the Spirit free to work in that person. What I take in the invisible I see the Spirit bring it to pass in the visible. I do not tell the person about the sin or that I have prayed. I just rejoice to see the Spirit working in that person, for I regard that person perfect in Christ, and that is how the Father sees him. The blood is greater than any sin. No sin is more powerful than the blood. The blood of Christ is just as powerful as it was 2000 years ago. I have received a lot of blessing from Andrew Murray's books, *The Blood of the Cross* and *The Holiest of All.* The blood of Christ is wonderful.

    I have seen Jesus. No, no vision but I have seen Him in the members of His body. When I first went to the Worldwide Evangelization Crusade, I loved to see how God supplied the material needs and also how He answered prayer: and in that I could say I saw God at work. Then the last few times I saw Him in the members of the W.E.C. Truly the foundation is Christ crucified, but the building is an habitation of God through the Spirit. One could see the various nationalities and the characteristics, but through them I saw the image of the Son. All bore the likeness of Him. Not by faith, but by visible sight I saw Him in His members. I can only say the King is all glorious within, for even though the bodies are mortal clay, His brilliance shown out through them, the eyes of the members all look alike. I often wondered what Jesus really looked like. He is altogether lovely and He has joined Himself to us.

I presume in Revelation 22 the bride now has her resurrected body. Yet what do we see? We are the living stones of which Christ is the chief cornerstone, and Christ also the Lamb within. Again it is the truth that Christ is head and body, and the Bride needs no light because the Lamb is in each one of the stones. We are the Bride, and the King is all glorious within us and manifests Himself through us to those without. He no longer pours water on us, but He Himself who is the WATER OF LIFE flows through us to those without. We are no longer hungry, because the BREAD OF LIFE feeds those without through us. The foundation stone is Christ, and, built upon that, are we living stones forming an habitation of God through the Spirit. The gate is of pearl, which symbolizes selling all He had to purchase us; and we His members consider Christ our Pearl, for which when we really get a glimpse of Him, we leave all to follow Him—head and body make One organism. I presume that this is a description of the Bride in resurrected bodies. Yet, we know that this body already is in the invisible in the sight of God. In Hebrews we are told we *are* come to Mount Zion, to the city of the Living God. In Revelation we see ourselves as that city itself, which is a habitation of God. Paul uses practical words, but John uses poetic words and has a different style. It is easy to see John's style in the Gospel, his Epistles and Revelation. He has a poet's style of describing things, such as Living Water, the Holy Spirit, the Lamb Jesus, etc. I am just beginning to realize that in Spirit we are in a timeless realm and spaceless. What I am seeing is that this Bride city or New Jerusalem which we look forward to *already is in the invisible,* because God is the Eternal I AM. As He regarded Christ slain from the foundation of the world and regarded it so in His dealing with the human race before it happened, cannot we also see ourselves now part of that City of Revelation 22 and draw on it, just as God regarded Christ slain before it came about in the visible? As far as I see, we are part of that glorious body without spot or wrinkle now. I realize that there is much Scripture to be fulfilled, some of which we are seeing fulfilled in our lifetime. We are part of that body, and the gates of hell could not and cannot prevail against it. God is just using history good or bad to bring about His purposes. In fact the history of the so-called future has already been written. God can just as easily use evil to bring about good, to bring about His purposes of reconciling all things in Christ."

To this I will add another remark recently made in a letter from another friend, and with that close the book: "I think I've got it. I see clearly now. I alone weak, foolish, inadequate; but then I see Christ in me, completely able, completely strong, completely wise. And it isn't Christ making me these things. I always remain I, but Christ in me always remains Christ. He never changes. I can't be all loving, all calm, etc., but He is. Thus I don't ask Him to make me that way, I ask Him to be Him in me."